Representative
Men of Japan

Kanzo Uchimura

July 27, 2021

Mr. Joe O'Brien,

You will see
Saigo's
hanging scroll
at our training
center.

Saban G.

装　　幀＝寄藤文平、阿津侑三

代表的
日本人
Representative
Men of Japan

Kanzo Uchimura
内村鑑三＝著

まえがき

　明治の知識人の心理は、現代人の欧米への意識の原点である。

　江戸時代に育まれた「上下関係」、「恩や義理」、「遠慮や謙遜」、「型への執着」、そして「精神的な鍛錬への美徳」などは、今の日本人の価値観の源となる。明治時代は、江戸時代がまだ近く、今以上に過去に培われた日本人の価値観への憧憬も深かった。

　　我々は今様々な変化にさらされ、ともすれば日本人独自の価値観の喪失に直面し、それにどのように対処すべきかと戸惑っている。例えば、戦後の民主主義の導入から70年を経て、より平等で公平で、かつガラス張りの制度を模索するなかで、不透明であるべき価値観への対処ができずに困惑している。

　内村鑑三は、そんな未来を予見したかのように、過去に日本人の意識構造を形作る上で重要な役割を果たした人々を描写した。その描写の方法には彼独自の国家観があって、事実をそのまま語るというよりも、日本という国が歩んできた道をより象徴的に表現する。西郷隆盛を解説するときに内村が記した「日本創造以来、時が熟すまで日本は鎖国するようにという天命があった」というくだりなどはその典型である。考えてみれば、それは的確な分析だ。戦

国時代にヨーロッパとの出会いがあり、古代には大陸との交流があったものの、日本はずっと島国で、確かにその中で鎖国してきたかのように独自の文明を築いてきた。

　江戸後期の名君上杉鷹山を紹介するくだりは、そんな著者の複雑な心理が、そのまま現代人の不安につながっていることを再確認させてくれる。「封建制度の欠点があったので、日本は立憲主義に変わった。しかし、それによって欠点以上のものを壊してしまったかもしれない」と内村鑑三は述懐する。失いつつある「忠誠心、武士道、そして情け深さ」という古来の価値観を彼は振り返る。

　今、我々は民主主義という制度に支えられた資本主義社会の中に生きている。日本人は、そんな社会の中にあって、ものごとを判断するときに天秤をバランスさせる片方の重みを失いつつある。片方は、法の元の公正さであり透明性である。しかし、もう片方にある「情け」という分銅が消滅しようとしている。その「情け」と「公正さ」との間を行き来し、社会という天秤をうまく機能させていた日本人の「融通」という発想が、年とともに希薄になっている。
　内村鑑三は、その近代国家の宿命ともいう、民主主義の中で逆に硬直する社会を、近代化した明治という時代を生きながら、予見していたのかもしれない。
　であればこそ、本書では、彼はあえて人を紹介し、その人の「情と徳」、そして自らの価値を貫く「信念」に光をあ

てている。そこに照らし出された人の姿は、現代社会から
してみれば矛盾を孕んでいるものの、その矛盾がゆえに、
そこから我々が今失いつつある知恵を再認識させてくれて
いるのである。

　明治時代、三人の賢人が日本を英文で紹介した。
　新渡戸稲造の「武士道」、岡倉天心の「茶の本」、そして
内村鑑三の「代表的日本人」がそれである。この３つの名
著は、奇しくも同じ頃に執筆される。その時代は日本が西
欧を手本にして近代化を成し遂げ、欧米列強の注目を集め
た時代であった。国家として成功するとき、人は自らの国
の文化や価値観を誇り、高らかと発信する。バブルたけな
わの80年代に、欧米とは一味違った日本人の経営スタイル
を日本の成功の秘訣と誇ったことを思い出せば、そんな大
衆心理が実際に躍動した事実を確認できる。
　しかし、明治の末期に日本人が誇りに思った価値観が国
家主義と一体となったとき、日本は破滅への坂を転がり落
ちた。そして昭和20年以降、再び日本人は欧米の思想や価
値観を復習し始めたのである。

　この日本人の心理の振り子をキリスト者であった著者は
見事に分析している。自らがキリスト者として欧米の文明
を学び、その倫理観や哲学観を習得してゆくなかで、逆に
自らのルーツによって支えられている自分自身を見つめ、
それを過去の人々を紹介する形で語ったのが本書なのだ。

であるから、内村はキリスト者でありながら、仏教や儒教に極めて寛容で、その宗教観をキリスト者である自分の中にも見出し、そこが欧米の人々と自らとを区別する多様さであると認識しているのだ。

　こうした視点で本書を読めば、明治の賢人の現代へのメッセージとしてそれを受け止めることができる。不透明な時代だからこそ、天秤のバランスの欠如に揺れる社会を、改めて見つめてゆきたいのである。

山久瀬　洋二

改訂版はしがき

　本書は、13年前の日清戦争中に書いた拙著『日本と日本人』の改訂版である。齢を重ねるうちに、故国に対する情熱は冷めたが、日本人の持つ素晴らしい性質には、**やはり感銘を受けずにはいられない**。私にとって日本は今でも、喜んで「祈りと、願いと、奉仕」を捧げる唯一の国なのだ。世界に日本人の素晴らしい性質を知ってもらいたい──ただし、**すでに有名になった忠誠心や愛国心以外の性質**を。これが本書の目的である。そして、この本が外国語で書く最後の書になることと思う。

内村鑑三

東京近郊、柏木にて

1908年　1月8日

PREFACE TO THE REVISED EDITION

This book is an edited version of my earlier work, *Japan and the Japanese*, which I wrote during the war with China thirteen years ago. Although my passion for my country has cooled as I've grown older, **I am still inspired** by the fine qualities of the Japanese people. Japan is still the only country to which I freely give "my prayers, my hopes, my service." I would like the world to see the fine qualities of the Japanese people—**qualities other than loyalty and patriotism, for which we are already famous**. This is the goal of this work, which I believe will be my last written in a foreign language.

Kanzo Uchimura
Kashiwagi, near Tokyo
January 8, 1908

初版はしがき

　本書に収めたエッセイのうち、2編はすでに出版したもので
あるが、日本の偉大な指導者たちを理解するうえでの助けと
なるよう、今回合わせて印刷することになった。外国語で書い
たものが、自国語で書く場合に比べて劣ることは承知してい
る。しかし、日本のことがこれほど外国人や旅行者によって書
かれている昨今、一度は**日本人が日本について書く**のも喜ば
しい変化といえるだろう。エッセイの内容のうちには、英語に
することによって意味が損なわれるものもあると思う。とは
いえ日本語が国際語となるまでは、**こういう試みもしばしば
必要だろう。**そういうわけで、英語の文法においてはいささか
の自信もないが、自分の望みと目的においては自信を持って、
本書をお届けする。

著者

日本、京都にて

黄海における海軍勝利の翌日

10

PREFACE TO THE FIRST EDITION

These essays, two of which have been published before, are now printed together to help us understand some of Japan's greatest leaders. I am aware that no work written in a foreign language is quite as good as when it is written in the author's own language. However, when so much written about Japan comes from outsiders and travelers, it is perhaps a welcome change for **a Japanese to write something on Japan** for once. I understand that some of the meaning of these essays will be lost in translation. However, until Japanese becomes a universal language, **attempts like this are often necessary**. So, with confidence only in my hopes and goals, and no confidence at all in my grammar, I give you these essays.

The Author

Kyoto, Japan

The Day after the Naval Victory in the Yellow Sea

目次

西郷 隆盛
新日本の創設者

Chapter 1
SAIGO TAKAMORI
A Founder of New Japan

第1節

1868年の日本の維新

　日本の国土が初めて海から現れた時、天はこう命じた。「日本よ、閉じこもれ。天がよいと言うまで、世界の他の国と交わってはならない」。そこで、この国は2千年間鎖国を続けた。日本の海を航海する外国船はなく、日本の海岸に足を踏み入れる外国人もいなかった。

　日本は**利己的な理由で鎖国したのではない。**人智を超えた力に命じられたのであり、そのおかげで、国がよりよく出来上がったのだ。鎖国は国にとって悪いものとは限らない。**危険に対する準備もないままに、自分の子を世間に送りだす父親がいるだろうか？**　たとえば、インドは世界のやり方を知らなかったため、たやすくヨーロッパの強欲の餌食となってしまった。

　この鎖国のおかげで、我が国独自の特質や文化を発達させることもできた。そのため、世界と接触するようになったときに、他国の文化の模倣になることはなかった。むしろ、独自の文化や

I.

The Japanese Revolution of 1868

When the land of Nippon first rose out of the ocean, the Heavens commanded, "Nippon, keep to yourself. Do not mix with the rest of the world until the Heavens say you are ready." So the country remained isolated for two thousand years. Foreign ships did not sail Japan's seas, and no foreigner set foot on Japan's shores.

Japan **did not isolate itself out of selfishness**. A higher power had ordered it, and the country was made better for it. Isolation is not always bad for a nation. **What father would send his child into the world without preparing her for its dangers?** India, for example, innocent of the ways of the world, fell easily to Europe's greed.

Our isolation also allowed us to develop our national character and culture. So, when we came into contact with the world, we were not made into a copy of other cultures. Instead, we retained our

慣習や個性を保ち続けたのだ。

　世界もまた、日本を正しく受け入れられるようになるまで、成長する時間が必要だった。1868年に起きた日本の明治維新が転機となって、東洋と西洋に**名誉ある関係**がもたらされたのだと私は信じている。日本が目覚める前は、世界の両側に調和はなかった。日本こそが、**ヨーロッパとアジアの間に正しい関係を築く**という問題を解決したのであり、現在もそれに努めているのである。

　こうして我が国の長い鎖国は終わったが、終わらせるためには適切な人材と機会が必要だった。日本では、最後にして最強の封建的権力者である幕府が、力を失いつつあった。国民たちは、国内の分裂や敵意にうんざりし、統一を求めている。これこそよい機会だったが、適切な人がこのような機会を利用することに気づく必要があった。

　米国海軍のマシュー・カルブレイス・ペリーは、世界でもっとも人類愛にあふれた人物のひとりだろう。彼の日記には、**自分は砲弾ではなく信仰によって、日本の海岸に衝撃を与えた**のだと書かれている。内向的なこの国を目覚めさせると

明治維新
江戸幕府から明治政府による天皇親政体制への転換とそれに伴う一連の改革。

江戸幕府
1603-1867、徳川家康が創設した武家政権。

マシュー・カルブレイス・ペリー
1794-1858、アメリカ海軍の軍人。1953年、浦賀へ来航。

own special culture, customs, and identity.

The world also needed time to evolve before it could receive Japan properly. I believe the Japanese Revolution of 1868 marks the point in time when the East and West were brought to ***honorable relations*** with each other. Before Japan awoke, there was no harmony between the two sides of the world. It is Japan that solved, and is solving, the question of **the *right relation* of Europe with Asia**.

Our country's long seclusion ended, but the right people and opportunities were needed to bring it to an end. In Japan, the last and greatest feudal dynasty was losing its power. The nation, tired of separation and hostility among its people, wanted unity. This was an opportunity, but the right man needed to know to use such an opportunity.

I consider Matthew Calbraith Perry of the United States Navy to be one of the greatest friends of humanity in the world. In his diaries we read that **he bombarded the shores of Japan with religion, not bullets**. His task of waking up a shy nation was

いう任務は難しかったが、ペリーは幸いにもやり遂げることができた。

　だが日本にも、ペリーとよく似た人物がいた。ペリーが外側からノックした時、1人の勇敢な大将が内側から答えたのだ。2人は顔を合わせたことがなく、互いに相手を賞讃したという話も聞かない。それでも文化の違いを超えて、彼らの心は瓜ふたつだった。それとは知らずに、ともに働いた。一方の提案を、他方が行動に移した。このようにして、**人智を超えた力は我々の運命を織りなす**のである。天の采配が行われている時、ただの人間である私たちにはその計画がわからない。しかし、思慮深い歴史家が過去を振り返り、出来事が織りなす模様を研究すると、私たちの目にもはっきりと見えてくるのである。

　このようにして、1868年の日本の明治維新は、あらゆる健全で持続する革命と同じく、必要に迫られて起こった。**強欲に対してかたくなに扉を閉ざしていた国が、正義と公平に対しては進んで開国したのである。**

日米和親条約
1854年に締結した条約により、日本は下田と函館を海港した。

difficult, but he was blessed in his work.

Perry had a counterpart in Japan. When Perry knocked from the outside, a brave general answered from within. The two men never saw each other, and we never hear of one complimenting the other. Yet despite their cultural differences, they were two similar souls. Without knowing it, they worked together. One put into action what the other proposed. In this way, **a Higher Power wove our Destiny**. We simple humans don't see Heaven's vision as it plays out, but it is revealed to us when a thoughtful historian looks back and studies the patterns and events.

Thus we see that the Japanese Revolution of 1868, like all healthy and lasting revolutions, was necessary. **The land that had been closed against greed freely opened itself to justice and equity**.

出生、教育、感化

西郷隆盛
1828-1877、武士、
軍人、政治家。

　「大西郷」は文政10年（1827年）、鹿児島の町に生まれた。薩摩藩という大きな藩の「中の下」の家の出である。6人兄弟——4人の兄弟と2人の姉妹——の長男だった。幼い頃は何も目立つところがなかった。おっとりした無口な少年で、友だちの中にはバカ呼ばわりする者さえいた。

　彼が初めて**義務感に目覚めた**のは、親戚のひとりが切腹するのを見たときである。その親戚は、まさに短刀を腹に突き刺す直前に、**命は主君と国に捧げるべきだ**と少年に語った。少年は涙にむせび、その時の記憶がいつまでも心に残った。

　西郷は大きな目と広い肩を持つ、太った大男に成長した。目が大きいので、「ウド（大きい）」という愛称で呼ばれた。相撲が大のお気に入りで、山を歩きまわるのが好きだった。中国の思想家、王陽明の著作に深く影響を受けた。禅の思想

王陽明
1472-1529、明代中
国の儒学者、思想
家。陽明学を起こ
した。

II.

Birth, Education, and Inspiration

"The Great Saigo" was born in the 10th year of Bunsei (1827) in the city of Kagoshima. He came from a "below middle" family in the large *han* of Satsuma. He was the eldest of six children—four brothers and two sisters. As a boy, there was nothing remarkable about him. He was a slow, silent boy— he was even called an idiot by some of his friends.

He first **awoke to a sense of duty** when he witnessed one of his relatives committing *hara-kiri*. The relative told the boy just before he plunged the dagger into his belly that **life must be devoted to master and country**. The boy wept, and this memory stayed with him.

Saigo grew up to be a big, fat man, with large eyes and broad shoulders. "Udo," the big-eyed, was his nickname. Wrestling was his favorite sport, and he liked to roam in the mountains. He was greatly influenced by the writings of the Chinese

もいくらか学んだが、ヨーロッパの文化は少しも習わなかった。このきわめて進歩的な日本人が受けた教育は、純粋に東洋的だったのだ。

陽明学の影響は、日本統一と「**ヨーロッパと対等な**」日本帝国という考えを西郷にもたらした。幕府が好んだ保守的な朱子学とは違い、陽明学は進歩的で、期待に満ち、未来に目を向けていた。キリスト教と似ている点が多いとよく言われている。キリスト教的なものが**日本の再構築の一翼を担った**という事実は、なかなか興味深いことである。

西郷のまわりの環境も、そういう考えが育つよう促したに違いない。国の南西端に位置する薩摩藩は、当時その方角からのみやってくるヨーロッパの影響を、いちばん近くで受けていた。また、外国との交易の中心である長崎に近いことも、大きく影響した。

そして、2人の同時代の人物が、西郷にもっとも大きな影響を与えた。1人は彼の主君、薩摩藩主の島津斉彬であり、もう1人は水戸藩の藤田東湖である。島津斉彬は大胆で、頭の切れる男であった。早くから、日本に変化が近づいているこ

島津斉彬
1809–1858、薩摩藩第11代藩主。幕末の名君と呼ばれたひとり。

藤田東湖
1806–1855、水戸藩士。水戸学の大家として、幕末の尊王志士たちに大きな影響を与えた。

philosopher Wang Yang Ming. He also studied some Zen philosophy, but he had no training in European culture. The education of this very progressive Japanese was purely Oriental.

Yang Ming philosophy influenced Saigo's ideas of a united Japan and a Japanese empire "**equal to Europe**." Unlike the conservative Chu philosophy preferred by the old governments, Yang Ming philosophy was progressive, full of promise, and focused on the future. Its similarity to Christianity has been noted often. It is an interesting fact that something like Christianity **played a part in the reconstruction of Japan**.

Saigo's environment also helped him develop his ideas. Located in the southwestern corner of the country, Satsuma stood nearest to European influence, which all came from that direction at the time. Its proximity to Nagasaki, a center of foreign commerce, was also influential.

Two living men influenced Saigo the most. One was his own feudal master, Shimazu Nariakira of Satsuma, and the other was Fujita Toko of the Mito *han*. Shimazu Nariakira was a confident and sharp man. Early on, he saw the changes coming

とを見通していた。西郷と島津は親友となり、祖国の未来について同じ意見を持っていた。

しかし、西郷にとっての最大の感化は、日本精神の師から与えられた。水戸の藤田東湖は、人の形をした日本そのものだった。東湖と西郷はまさに意気投合した。「私が胸に抱いている**計画を将来に伝えてくれる**のは、この若者しかいない」と、東湖は西郷について語っている。

そしておそらく、西郷が好きな山を歩きまわっているときに、天自らが彼に感化を与えたことにも触れておくべきだろう。森のしじまの中で、小さな声が、**おまえは使命を持って大地へ送られたのだ**とささやいた——それは国と世界の双方にとって重要な使命である。西郷は著作の中で何度も天について書いている。「天を相手にし、人を相手にするな。何事も天のために行なえ。他人を責めず、自分の誠の足らないところを探せ」。西郷はこういう言葉や、似たようなことを何度も語った。彼はこれを天から直接聞いたに違いない。

『南洲翁遺訓』
西郷隆盛の遺訓集。関係者が編纂し出版した。

upon Japan. Saigo and Shimazu were close friends, sharing similar views on the future of their country.

But Saigo's greatest inspiration came from a master of Japanese spirit. Fujita Toko of Mito *was* Japan in human form. Toko and Saigo got along perfectly. "Only that young man will **carry into the future the plans** that I now hold in my heart," Toko said of Saigo.

Perhaps we should also mention that Heaven itself influenced Saigo as he roamed his favorite mountains. In the silence of the forest, a small voice told him that **he was sent to earth with a mission**—a mission that was important to both his country and the world. Saigo mentions Heaven many times in his writings. "Deal with Heaven, and never with men. Do all things for Heaven's sake. Do not blame others; only search for a lack of sincerity in us." Saigo said these things and much more like it, and I believe he heard this directly from Heaven.

維新での役割

木戸孝允
1833–1877、長州藩
士、政治家。維新
志士時代の名は桂
小五郎。

大久保利通
1830–1878、薩摩藩
士、政治家。王政
復古の指導的役割
を果たした。

三条実美
1837–1891、公家、
政治家。明治政府
の中心人物のひと
り。

岩倉具視
1825–1883、公家、
政治家。明治憲法
の制定に尽力し
た。

月照
1813–1858、摂津国
大阪の僧侶。尊皇
攘夷運動に身を投
じた。

西郷は維新のほぼすべての役割に関与した。もちろん1人で国を建て直すことなど誰にもできない。他に多くの偉大な人物たちがこの仕事に参加した。それどころか、新しい日本の経済計画を立てる能力では、おそらく西郷がいちばん劣っていただろう。木戸や大久保のほうが、国政の問題を扱うのにずっと秀でていた。そして三条や岩倉のほうが、維新後の国を穏やかに安定させる点で、はるかに有能だった。**もしこれらの人物が1人でもいなかったら**、新しい帝国は今日のようではなかっただろう。とはいえ、**もし西郷がいなければ、はたして維新が可能だった**かどうか疑問である。日本には、維新の動き全体を始動させる力、そして形を与える人物が必要だった。これを提供したのが西郷だったのだ。

東湖に会ってまもなく、西郷は反徳川方についた。西郷の革命志向は、有名な活動家で仏僧の月照とともに自殺しようとしたとき、世間に知られることになる。徳川方に追われていたその僧

III.

His Part in the Revolution

Saigo was involved in almost every part of the Revolution. Of course, no one man can rebuild a nation, and many great men took part in this work. In fact, Saigo was perhaps the least competent in planning New Japan's economy. Kido and Okubo were much better at the details of internal administration, and Sanjo and Iwakura were far better than Saigo in drawing up the revolutionized country's peaceful settlement. The New Empire would not be what it is today **if it were not for *all* these men.** But I doubt **the Revolution would have been possible *without* Saigo.** We needed a force that could start the whole movement, someone to give it shape. Saigo provided this.

Soon after he met Toko, Saigo sided with the anti-Tokugawa party. Saigo's revolutionary ideas became public when he tried to commit suicide with the well-known activist and Buddhist priest

侶は、保護を求めて西郷のもとへやってきた。だが、彼を守ることができない西郷は、ともに自死することを提案した。月照は承知した。彼らは月夜の海へ出ていき、手に手を取って海へ飛びこんだ。そばにいた従者が水音を聞きつけ、2人の体を発見した。西郷は命を取りとめたが、月照は助からなかった。

この事件を見ると、西郷には**危険なほど優しい面のあった**ことがわかる。彼は友のために命を捨てるのをいとわなかった。この優しさが、後で見るように、最後に命取りとなるのである。

西郷は、この事件と他の反徳川活動のため流刑となった。しかし、1863年のイギリスによる砲撃の後に鹿児島に戻り、再び同じ道を歩み始める。彼は長州藩と徳川幕府の和平協定の締結に尽力した。ところが1年後、徳川幕府が長州征伐を始めたので、西郷は薩摩藩の兵を徳川方の援軍として送ることを拒否した。これが、有名な薩長同盟の始まりである。

西郷の流刑
一度目は奄美大島、二度目は徳之島（その後沖永良部島に遠島換え）に島流しされている。

長州征伐
1864年と1866年の二度にわたり、倒幕運動の拠点である長州藩攻撃のために起こした内戦。

長州征伐は失敗に終わった。そして薩長連合が、徳川幕府を倒せという天皇からの命令を受け

Gessho. The priest, who was running from Tokugawa men, went to Saigo for protection. But, unable to protect him, Saigo suggested they should both kill themselves. Gessho accepted. They went to the sea on a moon-lit night and jumped into the sea hand in hand. Nearby attendants heard the splash and found their bodies. Saigo lived, but Gessho did not.

In this incident, we see that Saigo **had a dangerously soft side**. He was willing to throw away his life for a friend. This softness would ultimately destroy Saigo, as we shall see.

Saigo was exiled for this incident and for other anti-Tokugawa activities. But when he returned to Kagoshima after the British bombardment of 1863, he picked up his old ways. He helped create a peaceful settlement between Choshu and the Tokugawa Government. But a year later, when the Tokugawa Government began the Choshu Invasion, Saigo refused to send Satsuma's troops to join Tokugawa. This was the beginning of the famous partnership between Satsuma and Choshu.

The Choshu Invasion failed. Then, on the day that the Satsuma–Choshu coalition received the

取ったまさにその日に、将軍が自ら進んで政権を放棄した。こうして**天皇は復権した**のである。

　連合軍はその後京都の町を制圧した。「12月9日の王政復古の大号令」が出され、徳川将軍は二条城を去った。1868年1月3日、伏見の戦いから戦争が始まった。官軍が勝利をおさめ、**その時から賊軍と呼ばれた徳川勢**は東へ逃れた。2つの大軍が後を追い、西郷は東海道軍を指揮した。4月4日、江戸城が官軍の手に落ちた。維新は成功したのである。

　これほど効果的な成功をもたらしたのは西郷だったが、彼は平和をも望んでいた。西郷の軍が品川まで進軍した時、戦場で旧友の勝海舟に出会った。友と戦った後、西郷は和平に向かう決心をした。西郷がこの決心をする数日前に、勝が西郷を愛宕山へ散歩に誘ったと言われている。足下に広がる「壮大な都市」を見おろして、西郷は深く心を打たれた。彼は友を振り返り、「もし我々が戦えば、きっとこの罪のない人々を苦しめることになるだろう」と言って、しばし沈黙した。

勝海舟
1823–1899、江戸生まれの武士、政治家。幕府側代表として、江戸無血開城を実現させた。

Emperor's orders to overthrow the Tokugawa dynasty, the Shogun freely gave up his authority. **The Emperor was reinstated**.

The coalition army then occupied the city of Kyoto. The "Grand Proclamation of the Ninth of December" was made, and the Tokugawa Shoguns left Nijo castle. On January 3, 1868, the war began with the battle of Fushimi. The imperialists were successful, and **the rebels, as the Tokugawa Party was now called**, fled to the east. Two great armies followed, with Saigo commanding the Tokaido branch. On April 4, the castle of Yedo fell to the imperialists. The Revolution had succeeded.

It was Saigo who brought about its success so effectively, but Saigo also desired peace. When his army marched to Shinagawa, he met an old friend, Katsu, in battle. After fighting his friend, Saigo decided to work toward bringing the country to peace. It is said that a few days before Saigo made this decision, Katsu took him up to Atago Hill for a friendly walk. Seeing "the magnificent city" under his feet, Saigo was deeply touched. He turned to his friend and said, "If we go to battle, I believe these innocent people will suffer," and was silent for a

西郷は強かったが、情に厚かった。**町は救われ、和平協議が行われた**。そして将軍は戦いを放棄し、江戸城を天皇に明け渡した。

　天皇が復権し国が統一されると、西郷は薩摩へ帰り、数年間、兵の訓練にあたった。彼にとって、戦いは終わっていなかった。国へ導入しようとしている大きな社会改革には、軍事力が必要なのである。だが首都に呼び戻され、維新の他の同志とともに参議（首席顧問官）という職に就いた。しかし悲しいことに、西郷が支持者を失うのは時間の問題だった。

moment.

Saigo was strong, but sympathetic. **The city was saved, peace was negotiated**, and the Shogun gave his castle to the Emperor.

With the Emperor back in power and the country united, Saigo returned to Satsuma for a few years and drilled soldiers. For him, the war had not ended. The great social reforms that were going to be introduced to the country needed force. But he was called back to the capital, where he took the office of *Sangi* (Chief Councilor) with other revolutionary men. But, sadly, it was just a matter of time before Saigo lost his followers.

朝鮮問題

　西郷は征服のためだけに戦争したかったのではない。**ヨーロッパの列強と肩を並べるために、**日本は領土を広げる必要があると感じたのだ。また、日本が東アジアにとって、**強いが寛容なリーダーになれる**という考えも持っていた。弱者を滅ぼしたいのではなく、むしろ導きたかったのだ。

　だが、これほど壮大な計画を持っていても、正当な理由なしに戦争するようなことはなかった。だから機会が訪れたときには、当然のように**天からの贈り物だと考えた**。西郷は朝鮮にその贈り物を見たのである。

李氏朝鮮
当時の執政者の興宣大院君は排外鎖国政策を推し進めた。

　日本にもっとも近い大陸の隣国である朝鮮は、**日本の新しい天皇を認めようとしなかった**。新政府から日本の使者が大使として送られたとき、朝鮮は公然と彼らを侮辱した。さらに在住する日本人を敵視し、厳しく扱う公布を出した。西郷は、そのような侮辱は無視できないと主張した。戦争を始めるほどではなかったが、朝鮮宮廷の非

IV.
The Korean Affair

Saigo did not want to go to war simply for conquest. He felt that for his country **to be equal with the Great Powers of Europe**, Japan needed to expand its territory. He also believed Japan **could be a strong but kind leader** to Eastern Asia. He did not want to destroy the weak, but rather to lead them.

However, even with all these grand ideas, he would not go to war without a proper cause for it. So, when an opportunity presented itself, he naturally **took it as a gift from Heaven**. Saigo saw such a gift in Korea.

Japan's nearest continental neighbor, Korea, **refused to acknowledge Japan's new emperor**. When Japanese envoys were sent by the new government to establish an embassy, Korea openly insulted them. Korea also treated Japanese residents with hostility and made a harsh order against them. Saigo argued that such insults could not be ignored.

礼をただすには十分だった。もし朝鮮がこれ以上日本人を侮辱するなら、その時は軍隊を送り、**日本は天が許すところまで征服の手を伸ばすだろう。**

国交修好全権大使
1873年、西郷は日韓の国交修好全権大使に任命される。

　おっとりした無口な西郷が、朝鮮への大使派遣の話になるといつも情熱的になった。自分を全権大使の長にしてほしいと、同僚たちに懇願した。その要求が聞きいれられると、彼は大喜びした。

　しかしこのとき、岩倉が、大久保や木戸とともに世界視察の旅から戻ってきたのである。彼らは世界で文明や、快適さや、幸福を目の当たりにしてきた。**西洋の力に圧倒された**岩倉たちは、1873年11月28日の朝鮮への大使派遣を取りやめる。今まで怒りを見せたことのない西郷が、この時ばかりは激怒した。腐った政府には金輪際関わらないと決意。辞表を机に投げつけ、東京を去って薩摩に帰った。そして西郷は、自らが創設の一助を担った政府に二度と加わることはなかった。

　朝鮮問題が終結したことで、政府の侵略政策は終わった。政府は「国内の発展」のほうに力を注ぐようになった。この政策の下で日本は文明

Although it was not enough to start a war, it was enough to demand justice at the Korean Court. If Korea further insulted the Japanese, then troops would be sent and Japan **would extend its conquest as far as Heaven would permit**.

The slow, silent Saigo was passionate whenever the Korean embassy was discussed. He begged his colleagues to make him the chief envoy. When his request was granted, he was overjoyed.

However, at this time, Iwakura returned with Okubo and Kido from their tour around the world, where they had seen civilization, comfort, and happiness. **Intimidated by the Western powers**, they canceled the Korean Embassy Act on November 28, 1873. Saigo, who had never shown anger before, went wild. He decided he would do nothing else with the rotten government. He threw his letter of resignation on the table, left Tokyo, and returned to Satsuma. He never again joined the government that he had helped establish.

The end of the Korean Affair also led to the end of the government's aggressive policies. The government became more focused on "internal

開化を迎えたが、同時に国は弱く、優柔不断に
なった。真のサムライ精神に反するようになっ
たのである。

development." Under these policies Japan saw much civilization, but the country also became weak and afraid of action. **We began to go against the true samurai spirit**.

第5節

謀反人としての西郷

西郷の人生でもっとも悲しい晩年については、多くを語る必要はないだろう。彼は政府に刃向う謀反人となった。なぜそうなったのか、さまざまな説がある。1つの説として、昔からの「優しさ」のせいで、謀反人たちに加わったというものがある。西郷を崇める約5千人の若者が、政府に公然と反抗したのだが、西郷は何も知らず、**しかも彼の意志に反していた**ようだ。反乱の成功は、西郷がその理由に自身の名前と威光を与えるかどうかにかかっていた。西郷は最強の男だったが、**どうしてもと懇願されることには弱かった。**20年前にも、1人の仏僧のために自死しかけたのだ。今再び、彼は生徒たちとの友情のために、命と名誉を犠牲にしようと心に決めたのかもしれない。

西郷はまた、政府に対してひじょうに不満を持っていた。ことによると、人生最大の目的を達成することができずに失望し、反乱に身を投じたのかもしれない。1868年の維新は、彼の理想

私学校党
西郷は鹿児島に私学校を設立。士族とその子弟の若者たちが私学校党を形成し、県下最大の勢力となった。

V.

Saigo as a Rebel

We don't need to say much about this final and saddest part of Saigo's life. He became a rebel against his government. There are many theories as to why he did so. One theory is that his old "softness" caused him to join the rebels. Some five thousand young men who worshipped Saigo openly rebelled against the government, seemingly **without his knowledge and against his will**. Their success depended upon his giving his name and influence to their cause. Although Saigo was of the strongest of men, he **was weak before the requests of the needy**. Twenty years ago he had almost killed himself for a Buddhist priest. Now, again he might have been convinced to sacrifice his life and honor out of friendship with his students.

Saigo was also dissatisfied with the government. Perhaps we can say that he participated in the rebellion because he was disappointed in his life's greatest goals. The Revolution of 1868 had

とは正反対の政府を生み出してしまったからだ。だが理由はどうあれ、彼は反乱軍に加わったのである。

西郷は戦争中それほど活躍したわけではない。他の者たちがすべての戦略を練った。彼らは1877年の2月から9月まで戦ったが、**望みが打ち砕かれる**と、「先祖の墓」に入るため、なんとか鹿児島まで戻った。その地の城山で、政府軍に取り囲まれるなか、西郷は**上機嫌で**碁を打っていた。そして従者の1人を振り返ると、「いつか私が畑から帰る途中に、下駄の鼻緒をすげてやったのは、おまえではなかったか？」と言った。男はそのときのことを思い出し、自分だと認めて、許しを乞うた。「なに、かまわん！」と西郷は答えた。「ちょっとからかってみただけだ」

これは本当の出来事である。**大将が2人の若者の命令に従ったのだ。**若者たちは薩摩の風習にならって、出会った農夫なら誰にでも下駄の鼻緒をすげさせるという侍の特権を使った。このときのその農夫がたまたま大西郷であり、彼は一言の文句も言わずにその仕事をしたのだ。西郷ほど謙虚な人物は他にいないだろう。

1877年9月24日の朝、政府軍は城山を攻撃し

西南戦争
1877年、私学校党を中核とする九州の士族が西郷隆盛を擁して起こした反政府内戦。

produced a government that was the opposite of his ideal. Whatever his reasons, he united with the rebels.

He was not active in the war. Others looked after all the battle strategies. They fought from February to September 1877, and when **their hopes were shattered**, they forced their way back to Kagoshima to be buried in their "fathers' graveyard." There, at Castle Hill, while government forces gathered all around, Saigo played *go* **in the best of spirits**. Turning to one of his attendants, he said, "Aren't you the one whose wooden shoes I mended one day, as I was returning from my farm?" The man remembered the occasion, confessed, and asked for forgiveness. "It is nothing!" replied Saigo. "I am just teasing."

It was true. **The General did obey the demands of two youths**, who, according to a custom in Satsuma, used the right of the samurai to have his shoes fixed by any farmer he happened to meet. The farmer in this case happened to be the great Saigo, who did the job without a single complaint. No one was more humble than Saigo.

On the morning of September 24, 1877, the

た。西郷が仲間とともに敵に向かおうとしたとき、一発の弾丸が腰に当った。まもなく反乱軍の少数の隊は全滅し、西郷の遺体は敵に奪われた。「遺体を丁重に扱え」と、敵方の大将の1人が叫んだ。「なんと穏やかな顔だろう！」と、他の者が言った。**西郷を討ち取った全員が泣いた**。そして涙を流しながら彼を葬った。その墓は今日でも、涙とともに訪れる人が絶えない。このようにして、もっとも偉大で最後のサムライがこの世を去ったのである。

南洲神社
1880年、墓参りに訪れる人が多いため、西郷隆盛を祭神する神社が設けられた。

government attacked Castle Hill. Saigo was meeting the enemy with his comrades when a bullet struck his hip. Soon the little group of rebels was destroyed, and the enemy took Saigo's body. "Treat that body with respect," cried one of the enemy's generals. "What a kind face he has!" said another. **Those who killed him all wept**. They buried him with tears, and his tomb is visited with tears to this day. This is how the greatest and the last of the samurai died.

西郷の生活と人生観

「児孫のために美田を買わず」
西郷が詠んだ漢詩の一節。西郷は遺産を遺さなかった。謀反人として討たれたにも関わらず、西郷の遺族は国からの援助を受けた。

　西郷の祖国に対する貢献の影響を完全に評価するには、まだ時が早すぎるが、彼がどういう人物であったかを知るための情報は十分にある。まず第一に、**西郷はことのほか謙虚であった**。日本軍の最高司令官であり、有力な閣僚でありながら、外見は一般の兵士と変わらなかった。生活費は15円しか使わず、月給の残りは貧しい友人たちに与えた。東京の番町にある家はみすぼらしいものだった——家賃はたったの月3円である。普段の服装は、薩摩絣（さつまがすり）の着物に平織の帯で、大きな下駄を履いていた。彼は宮中の晩餐会（ばんさんかい）でも、他のあらゆる場所と変わらず、このような姿で現れた。

　西郷のたった1つの趣味は、犬だった。贈り物は通常受け取らなかったが、**犬に関するものならなんでも喜んで受け取った**。犬は彼にとって生涯の友だった。夜も昼も、犬と一緒に山の中で過ごすことが多かった。孤独だった彼は、その孤独を分け合う友として犬を連れていたのだ。

VI.

His Ways of Living and Views of Life

Although it is too soon to fully measure the impact of Saigo's service to his country, we have enough information to know what kind of man he was. First of all, **Saigo was extremely humble**. Although he was commander-in-chief of the Japanese army and an influential cabinet-member, his appearance was that of a common soldier. All his needs cost just fifteen yen, and he gave the rest of his salary to his poor friends. His house in Bancho, Tokyo, was shabby—the rent was *three yen a month*. His usual clothing was Satsuma-made cotton with a calico *obi*, and large wooden clogs. He appeared like this at the Imperial dinner table as everywhere else.

He had one hobby, and that was dogs. Although he didn't normally accept gifts, he received **anything dog-related** with gratitude. His dogs were his friends throughout his life. He often spent days and nights with them in the mountains. A lonely man, he had dogs to share his loneliness.

西郷は言い争いが大嫌いで、**できるだけ避け
ようとした**。あるとき宮中の宴会に招かれ、いつ
もの質素な服装で出席した。ところが帰ろうと
すると、下駄がなかった。そのようなことで誰を
も煩わせたくなかったので、雨の中を裸足で歩い
て出た。門まで来ると、門番に呼び止められ、何
者かと尋問された。「西郷大将だ」と彼は答えた。
だが門番は信用せず、通そうとしない。そこで西
郷は雨の中に立ったまま、自分の身元を門番に
保証してくれる人が通るのを待った。まもなく
岩倉大臣の乗った馬車が近づいてきた。裸足の
男は大将だと判明し、大臣の馬車に乗せられ、運
ばれていった。

　西郷をそばで見ていた人が、彼の私生活につ
いて次のように語っている。「私は13年間一緒に
暮らしましたが、使用人を叱るのを見たことがあ
りません。布団の上げ下ろしをし、窓を開け、他
のこまごました用事も自分でやりました。でも、
**他の人がやってあげても嫌がりはしませんでし
た**。手伝ってくれるというなら断りません。子ど
ものように純粋な人でした」

　このように彼の生活は謙虚で質素だった。し
かし、彼の思想は聖人や哲学者のものである。

He disliked arguments and **avoided them at all costs**. Once he was invited to an Imperial feast, which he attended in his usual plain clothes. When he was leaving, he could not find his clogs. Because he did not want to trouble anybody about them, he walked out barefoot in the rain. When he came to the gate, the guard stopped him and demanded to know who he was. "General Saigo," he replied. But they did not believe him and wouldn't let him pass. So he stood in the rain waiting for somebody who might identify him to the guard. Soon a carriage approached with Minister Iwakura in it. The barefooted man was proved to be the general, was taken into the minister's coach and carried away.

One witness said this about Saigo's private life: "I lived with him thirteen years and I never saw him scolding his servants. He made his bed, opened his windows, and took care of his other personal chores. But **when others did them for him, he never interfered**; and he didn't decline help when offered. He was as pure as a child."

This was how he lived, humbly and simply. But his thoughts were like those of a saint and a

敬天愛人
道は天地自然の
物にして、人はこ
れを行うものなれ
ば、天を敬するを
目的とす。天は我
も同一に愛し給ふ
ゆえ、我を愛する
心を以て人を愛す
る也。

「天を敬い、人を愛する（敬天愛人）」という言葉が、彼の考えを要約している。「人は自分に打ち勝つことで成功し、自分を愛すれば失敗する」と西郷は言った。彼が神や天についてどう考えていたかはわからないが、その行動と言葉から、天は全能であり、天の法は情け深いと信じていたことがわかる。そして、人は誠実な心によってのみ、天に近づくことができると考えていた。

西郷にとって、**正義ほど大切なものはなかった**。自分の命や祖国でさえも、正義ほど重要ではなかった。彼はこう言っている。「**正義の道を歩もうとし、正義のためなら祖国とともに死ぬほどの覚悟がなければ**、外国の列強とよい関係を持つことはできない。もし相手の強大さを恐れ、和平を懇願し、相手の望みをすべてのむなら、**弱く取るに足らぬ者に見えるだけ**だ。友好的な関係を失い、列強の奴隷となるであろう」

西郷は著作を残さなかった。しかし多くの詩と、数編の随筆が残っている。多くの日本の学者と違って、彼の言葉はこれ以上ないほど簡潔である。たとえば、次のような詩がある。

philosopher.

"**Revere Heaven; love people**," summed up his views. "A man succeeds by overcoming himself, and fails by loving himself," Saigo said. We don't know what he thought of God or Heaven, but his words and actions show that he believed Heaven was all-powerful, and that its Laws were kind. And he believed one could only get close to Heaven with a sincere heart.

To Saigo **there was nothing so precious as righteousness**. Not even his life or his country was more precious than righteousness. He says: "We cannot have good relations with foreign powers **unless we want to walk in righteousness, and even fall with our country if it is the righteous thing to do**. If we are afraid of their greatness, beg for peace, and follow all their wishes, **we will only seem weak and unimportant**. We will lose our friendly relations, and we will become their servants."

Saigo left us no books. But he left us many poems and several essays. Unlike many Japanese scholars, his words are the simplest that can be imagined. For example:

我に千糸の髪あり

さんさんとして漆より黒し

我に一片の心あり

こくこくとして雪より白し

わが髪はなお絶つべし

我が心は截つべからず

また山を歌った詩の中に、このような箇所がある。

地古く、山高く

夜よりも静かなり

人語を聞かず

ただ天を看るのみ

　西郷は日本でもっとも偉大な人物のひとりだと、私は信じている。ただ彼の偉大さは、持って生まれた才能や、真に天才的なものではなかった。そうではなくて、意志の力が彼の偉大さに深く関係していたに違いない。西郷の偉大さは、道徳的なものであった。**健全な道徳的基盤の上に、祖国を建て直そうとした**のであり、この意味で、西郷はある程度成功したのである。

"Hair I have of thousand strings,
  Darker than the lacquer.
A heart I have an inch long,
  Whiter than the snow.
My hair may divided be,
  My heart shall never be."

Or this part of a mountain-song of his:

"Land high, recesses deep,
  Quietness is that of night.
I hear not human voice,
  But look only at the skies."

I believe Saigo is one of Japan's greatest men, but his greatness is not of natural talent or true genius. No, I believe will power had a lot to do with his greatness. His greatness was of the moral kind. **He tried to rebuild his nation upon a sound moral foundation**, and in this, he partially succeeded.

第**2**章

上杉鷹山
封建領主

Chapter 2
UESUGI YOZAN
A Feudal Lord

第1節

封建制度

立憲主義
憲法に基づいて
政治を行い、支配
者の権力を制限し
ようという政治原
則。

封建主義
封土の授受を基礎
とし、領主とその
臣下との主従関係
を社会構造の基本
とするやり方。

私たちは残酷な政治形態を終わらせるため、民主主義のような制度を作ってきたが、いかなる制度であっても、美徳に取って代われるものはないとわかっている。封建制度には欠点があったので、日本は立憲主義に変わった。しかしそれによって、欠点以上のものを壊してしまったのかもしれない。封建主義とともに、忠誠心、武士道、そして情け深さも失ったのだ。

本当の意味での忠誠心とは、君主と家臣がお互いじかに接しているときにこそあり得るものだ。**両者の間に「制度」を持ちこめば、忠誠心は失われる**。献身とその美しさはすべて、仕えるべきわが君主と、慈しむべきわが家臣がいる時に生まれるのだ。封建制度の強みは、**支配する者とされる者の間のこの人間的な関係**にある。要するに、家族制度がそのまま国家に適応されていたわけだ。だから、もし完全な形であれば、封建制度は理想的な政治形態だろう。なぜなら、どのような法律や制度でも、愛の律法に勝るものは

I.

The Feudal Form of Government

Although we have created systems, such as democracy, to end cruel forms of government, we know that no system can take the place of virtue. Feudalism had its flaws, so Japan replaced it with constitutionalism. But by doing so, **we may have destroyed more than just its flaws**. Together with feudalism, we have lost loyalty, chivalry, and much kindness.

Loyalty in its true sense is only possible when the master and the subject are in direct contact with each other. **If you bring a "system" between the two, loyalty is lost.** Self-sacrifice and all its beauty exist when I have *my* master to serve, or *my* subject to care for. The strength of feudalism lies in **this *personal* relation between the governor and the governed.** In its essence it is really the family system applied to a nation. Therefore, in its perfect form, it is the ideal form of government, because no law or constitution is better than the Law of

ないからである。

　おそらく数千年後には、完璧な政治形態が地上にもたらされるだろう。だがそのようなものを待ち望む間に、ひじょうによく似たものを思い出すことにしよう。それがこの地上に——しかも異教の国の日本に——存在したのである。そう、西洋から知恵が伝わる前に、**この国は平和の道を知っていたのだ。**

Love.

Perhaps after several thousand years have passed, we will have a perfect form of government on earth. But while we wait for such a thing, let's remember something very much like it. It existed on this earth—and in heathen Japan, at that. Yes, before wisdom came from the West, **this land knew the ways of peace**.

人と事業

上杉鷹山
1751–1822、出羽国
米沢藩の第9代藩
主。

　今の羽前にあたる米沢藩を継いだとき、鷹山は17歳の少年だった。九州の小大名である秋月家に生まれたが、実家より格上で領地も大きい上杉家の養子となった。しかしこの養子縁組が後に、日本史上もっとも困難な試練を彼にもたらしたのである。

細井平洲
1728–1801、尾張国
（名古屋）出身の儒
学者。

　少年の叔母が先代の米沢藩主に、「物静かで思慮深い」少年として彼を推薦した。他にも大勢いた身分の高い家の子たちと違って、鷹山は師である細井を心から尊敬した。また感受性の強い少年だったので、信仰深くもあった。米沢藩主となったときには、守護神と信じる春日神社へ次のような誓約文を送った。

「1.　学問と武術の修練を怠らないこと。

　2.　民の父母となることを第一とすること。

II.
The Man and His Work

Yozan was a boy of seventeen when he inherited the territory of Yonezawa in today's province of Uzen. Born to the Akizuki family, a rather small *daimyo* of Kyushu, he was adopted by the Uesugi, who were higher in rank and owned more territory. But the adoption later presented him with one of the most difficult challenges of Japanese history.

The boy's aunt recommended him to the elder lord of Yonezawa as a "quiet and meditative" boy. Unlike many other sons of nobility, he deeply respected his tutor, Hosoi. And, as a sensitive boy, Yozan was religious as well. On the day he took office as the head of Yonezawa, he sent the following promise to the temple of Kasuga, his guardian god:

"I.   I shall never neglect my exercises, literary and military.

"II. To be a father and a mother to my people shall be my first priority.

3. 日夜、次の言葉を忘れないこと。

ぜいたくなければ危険なし
施して浪費するなかれ

4. **言行不一致、不正、不実、不作法**をしない
よう注意すること。

もしこれらの誓約を怠るなら、神罰が下り、家
運が永遠に消し去られますように。

上杉弾正

藤原治憲

明和4年 （1767年）8月1日」

弾正大弼
当時の監察・警察
機構の上級ポスト
のひとつ。

藤原治憲
「藤原」は上杉氏の
姓、「治憲」は隠居
して鷹山を名乗る
前の名。

　上杉家は全国でも最強の藩のひとつだったが、
会津地方へ移された時、その力が大きく削られ
た。その後、関ヶ原の戦い（1600年）で反徳川方
についたため、藩は再び移された。今度は遠く離
れた米沢の地である。石高は30万石に減封され
た。それから、さらに半分に減らされた。鷹山が
藩主となった時、上杉家は15万石の大名だった
が、家臣や慣習は100万石でまかなっていた頃の

"III. Day and night, I will never forget these words:

No extravagance, no danger.

Give in charity, but waste not.

"IV. I shall guard myself from **inconsistency, injustice, unfaithfulness, and indecency.**

If I ever neglect these promises, let divine punishment strike me down, and the family fortune be forever consumed.

Uesugi, of the Office of *Danjo*,
Fujiwara Harunori
The First Day of the Eighth Month of the Fourth
Year of Meiwa (1767)"

The Uesugi clan had been one of the most powerful in the whole country, but when the clan was moved to the Aizu district, its power was greatly reduced. Then, when the clan sided with the anti-Tokugawa party in the battle of Sekigahara (1600), the clan was moved again, this time to the remote district of Yonezawa. Their revenue was reduced to 300,000 *koku*. Then their revenue was

ままだった。新しい領地では、とうてい藩を支えることができない。借金は数百万両あり、全領内で人々が貧困にあえいでいた。

米沢の地には海岸がなく、土地はやせ、天然の資源も乏しかった。**やがて藩が崩壊し、領民が破産する**のは間違いないと思えた。藩は5両の金さえ工面できなかったのだ。若き鷹山の仕事は、**まずこの状態に歯止めをかけ**、せめて耐えられるものに回復させることだった。そして、もし守護神の春日明神がさらに祝福してくれるなら、自分の領地を、昔の賢人が語った理想の国にすることが目標となった。

春日明神
春日神社の祭神
で、上杉家の氏神。

鷹山が初めて米沢の領地に入ったのは、藩主になって2年後である。行列が貧しい村から貧しい村へと通り過ぎていくとき、若き藩主の多感な心はひどく揺さぶられた。その旅中のあるとき、彼が火鉢の炭に息を吹きかけているのを従者たちが目にした。

「殿、すぐに火をお持ちいたします」と1人が言った。

cut again by half. When Yozan became chief, the Uesugi was a *daimyo* of 150,000 *koku*, but with all the subjects and habits that were once supported by 1,000,000 *koku*. The new territory, then, barely supported the clan. Its debts totaled millions, and people were impoverished throughout the district.

The district of Yonezawa has no seacoast, and its fertility and natural resources are very poor. It seemed certain that **the clan would dissolve and its people would go bankrupt**. The clan could not even raise five pieces of gold together. Young Yozan's business was first **to put a stop to this state of things**, then to restore it to something tolerable. Then, if his guardian god Kasuga would bless him even more, his goal was to make his territory an *ideal state* described by the old philosophers.

Yozan first entered his territory of Yonezawa two years after he took office. As the procession passed poor village after poor village, the sensitive heart of the young chief was touched. At one point during this visit, his attendants saw him blowing at a charcoal fire in a *hibachi*.

"We'll give your Lordship fire," one said.

「いや、今はよい」鷹山は答えた。「すばらしい教訓を学んでいるところなのだ。後で教えてやろう」

その夜、行列が宿に泊まったとき、藩主は従者を集めて教訓の説明をした。彼はこう語った。「民の悲惨な姿を見て絶望していたとき、目の前の小さな炭火が目に入った。それは今にも消えようとしていた。だが、そっと取り上げて、**やさしく辛抱強く息を吹きかけると、火をよみがえらせることができた**。私は自分に、『同じようにして、わが領地と民をよみがえらせることができるだろうか？』と問うた。すると、再び希望がわいてきたのだ」

"Not now," Yozan replied, "I am learning a great lesson. I will tell you what it is later."

When the procession stopped for the night, the chief called his attendants together and explained the lesson. He said, "As despair took hold of me, as I witnessed my people's miseries, I saw a little charcoal fire before me. It was on the point of going out. I slowly took it up, and **by blowing at it gently and patiently, I succeeded in bringing the fire back to life**. I asked myself, 'May I bring my land and people back to life in the same way?' and I felt hopeful again."

第3節

行政改革

　他人を変えるには、まず自分から変えなければならない。もちろん、最初に解決すべき問題は財政だった。米沢藩を**回復させる**には、**もっとも厳しい倹約を行うしかない**。鷹山は、1050両かかっていた家計の支出を209両に削減した。屋敷内の女中も、以前は50人だったのを9人に減らした。木綿の着物しか身につけず、毎食一汁一菜しか食べなかった。また家臣にも倹約するよう命じた。毎年の手当ては半分に減らされ、このようにして節約した金が借金の返済に充てられた。借金から解放されるまで、これを16年間続けなければならなかったのだ！

　適材適所なしに良い政治はできない。そこで鷹山は優秀な人材を探し出した。藩の乏しい財源から、有能な人物には十分な手当を支払った。そして、この人々を3つの異なる役職に分けて、民の上に配置した。まず第1に、郷村頭取とその下の役人たちがいた。彼らは「民の父母」であり、

III.

Administrative Reform

Change in others must begin with change in one's self. Naturally, finance was the first question to be settled. The district of Yonezawa **could only be restored by the strictest frugality.** Yozan cut his family expense of 1,050 pieces of gold to 209 pieces. He kept only nine maids in his household instead of fifty as before. He wore nothing but cotton and ate no more than soup and one dish at each meal. He also ordered his subjects to be economical. Annual allowances were cut in half, and all savings went to paying off debt. This had to be continued for *sixteen years* before the clan could be free from debt!

No good government is possible **without the right men in the right places**, so Yozan found good men. Out of his small treasury, he paid able men well. He placed these men over his people in three different classes. First, there were the governor and his officers. These were the "fathers and mothers

小藩の行政を監督した。鷹山はこの役職の者たちに、誠実であれと命じた。「**誠実は愛を生み、愛は知恵を生む**」と彼は語った。

第2の役職は説教師で、民に「親孝行、思いやり、結婚のこと、身だしなみ、食物と食事作法、葬式、家の修理など」について教えた。全領地が12の地区に分けられ、各地区に民を導く説教師（教導出役<ruby>教導出役<rt>きょうどうしゅつやく</rt></ruby>）がおかれた。この教導出役たちは年に2回集まり、情報を交換して藩主に報告した。

第3の役職は警察（<ruby>廻村横目<rt>かいそんよこめ</rt></ruby>）である。彼らは民の犯罪を取り調べ、厳しく罰した。**情け容赦なく**、村の**隅々までで**くまなく調べ上げた。

3つの役割は互いにうまく機能した。郷村頭取とその下の役人が全体的な政策を維持する一方で、鷹山はこう言った。「**教育のない民を治めるのは手間がかかり、効果もあがらない**」。そこで教導出役が教育を施した。だが、**規律のない教育も効果がない**。そのため厳しい警察制度が規律を与えたのである。

of the people," who managed the administrative duties of the little state. Yozan ordered this class of officers to be sincere. "**Sincerity begets love, and love begets knowledge**," he told them.

The second class of officers were preachers who taught the people "filial piety, charity, matters of marriage, decency in clothing, food and ways of eating, funeral services, house-repairs, etc." The territory was divided into twelve districts for this purpose, each with a head bishop over it. These bishops met twice a year to share knowledge and to report to the chief.

The third class was the police. They investigated people's crimes and punished them severely. They **showed no mercy** and looked into **every nook and corner** of the villages.

The three functions worked well together. While the governor and administrators upheld general policies, Yozan said, "**To rule an uneducated people is costly and ineffective**." So, his bishops provided that education. But **education without discipline is also ineffectual**. So, the strict police system provided discipline.

新しい制度は5年間、なんの問題もなく行われた。法と秩序が村に広がり、民は再び希望を持ち始めた。ところがそのとき、変化を恐れる人々が反逆したのである。

ある日、藩の重臣7人が若き藩主のもとへやってきて、新しい政治制度をやめるよう説得した。しかし鷹山は、**民に決めさせよう**と決心した。もし民が新体制に反対なら、彼は進んで藩主を辞するつもりだった。

鷹山は家臣全員を招集した。何千人もの家臣が城に集まると、鷹山は、**自分の政治が天意に反していると思うか**と尋ねた。郷村頭取とその下の役人たちが「いいえ」と言った。警察が「いいえ」と言った。隊長と隊士たちも「いいえ」と言った。鷹山は満足した。そして7人の重臣を自分の前に呼び、裁きを下した。彼らのうち5人は土地と財産の半分を没収され、首謀者の2人は侍の作法に従って罰せられた──つまり切腹である。

批判者はこれを最後にいなくなり、新制度はさらに向上していった。そして鷹山は、この民に繁栄をもたらすことに取りかかった。

The new system operated for five years without any trouble. Law and order increased in the villages, and people began to have hope again. But then, people who feared change rebelled.

One day, seven of the district's highest officials came to the young chief and tried to convince him to stop his new system of government. But Yozan **decided that he would let his people decide**. If *they* objected to the new administration, he would willingly step down as chief.

Yozan called a meeting of all his subjects. Thousands gathered in the castle, and Yozan asked **if they felt his administration went against Heaven's will**. The governor and his officers said, "No." The police said, "No." The captains and sergeants said, "No." Yozan was satisfied. He called the seven officials before him and sentenced them. Five of them were made to give up half of their land and wealth, while the two leaders were punished according to the law of samurai—with *hara-kiri*.

When the critics were gone once and for all, the system continued to improve, and Yozan went on to create prosperity for this people.

第4節

産業改革

　鷹山には2つの産業政策があった。(1) 領内に**荒れ地を残さないこと**と、(2) 民のうちの**怠け者をなくす**ことである。この政策を行なえば、きっと15万石の領地から30万石収穫できると鷹山は考えた。そのため、全身全霊で農業を奨励した。

　平時には侍も農民として働かせて、荒れ地を数千エーカーの耕地によみがえらせた。また、漆の木を植えるよう命じた。武家はそれぞれ15本、他の家は5本、寺は20本植えるよう求められた。割り当て以上に植えると、1本につき20セントの報奨金が出た。枯らしたまま植え替えずにいると、同額の罰金が科された。このようにして、100万本を超える貴重な木が、またたく間に植えられた。**後世の者たちは、これから大きな利益を得た。**

1エーカー
およそ4047平方
メートル、1200坪。

　しかし、鷹山の主な目的は、領地を最大の絹の

IV.

Industrial Reforms

Yozan had two industrial policies: (1) **leave no wasted land** in his territory, and (2) **have no laziness** among his people. With these policies, Yozan believed he could make his land produce 300,000 *koku* instead of 150,000. He encouraged agriculture with his whole heart.

By turning his samurai into farmers in times of peace, Yozan recovered thousands of acres from wilderness. He ordered lacquer-trees to be planted. Every samurai family was required to plant 15 trees; every family other than samurai, 5; and every temple, 20. For every one tree that was planted above the required number, he gave a reward of twenty cents; and for every one that died and was not replaced, a fine of the same sum was charged. Thus, over one million trees of these valuable trees were planted within a very short time. **Future generations benefited from this greatly**.

But Yozan's chief aim was to make his territory

産地にすることだった。この資金のため、自分の家計をさらに切り詰めた。そして50年という長い年月の後、彼が植えた数千株の桑の木は増え育ち、全領地にもう植えるところがなくなってしまった。米沢産の絹といえば、今では市場の最高級品である。

鷹山はまた、**かんがい施設によって、不毛な土地を肥沃な土地に変えた**。最貧の大名が、昔の日本で最高に素晴らしい土木工事のうちの2つを行うことができたのだ。1つは高架橋による水路網で、28マイルの距離まで水を運んだ。もう1つは、1200フィートの水のトンネルである。これらが完成すると、鷹山の領地に豊かな実りが訪れた。今日まで、東北地方で米沢だけが**干ばつの被害を受けたことがない**。

鷹山はさらに、領地に良馬を持ち込み、池や川に魚やウナギを飼い、炭鉱夫や織工を他の地方から招いて、領地内のあらゆる資源を発展させた。民のうちの怠け者を働き者に変えることで、**国でもっとも貧しい地方を模範的な多産の地に変えたのである**。

桑
絹を生産するカイコの餌となる作物。

1マイル
およそ1.6キロメートル。28マイルはおよそ45キロメートル。

1フィート
およそ30センチメートル。1200フィートはおよそ366メートル。

one of the greatest silk-producing districts. To fund this, he again cut his family expenses. After fifty long years, the few thousand mulberry bushes he planted grew and multiplied, and his whole territory had no more space left for them. The Yonezawa silk brand is now the best in the market.

Yozan also **turned his barren territory into a fertile one with irrigation systems**. The poorest *daimyo* was able to build two of the most remarkable engineering works ever undertaken in Old Japan. One was a network of viaducts that transported water for twenty-eight miles. The other was a water tunnel of 1,200 feet. After their completion, fertility flowed into Yozan's territory. To this day, Yonezawa is the only northern province that **does not suffer from drought**.

Yozan also imported better horses into his district, stocked ponds and streams with fish and eels, invited miners and weavers from other provinces, and developed all the resources of his territory. By turning the lazy among his people into hard workers, he **turned the poorest district in the land into an example of productivity**.

第5節

社会改革と道徳改革

　東洋思想の美徳のひとつは、経済を道徳の一部とみなすことである。健康な木に実がなるように、徳が富をもたらすのだ。これが、鷹山のあらゆる改革でいちばん良いところだろう。彼の主要な目的は、**民を有徳な人々にすること**だった。富そのものを目的として重視したのではなく、**文明を作り上げるために富が必要だった**のである。

　藩主になってから数年後、藩校を再び開校した。興譲館、つまり「謙譲の徳を振興する所」と名付けた。当時最高の学者のひとり、細井平洲（鷹山の師）が館長を務めた。その学校は、貧しい者も高等教育を受けられるよう、多くの奨学金を無償で与えた。

興譲館
1697年に設置された学問所を1776年に再建した。

　どれほど良い政治でも、病人を治す施設がなければ完成とはいえない。このことでも、鷹山には解決策があった。医学校を開校し、薬草を育てるための植物園を開いた。さらに数人の西洋医

好生堂
1789年創立。蘭学医として著名な杉田玄白の新しい医学が取り入れられた。

V.
Social and Moral Reforms

One beautiful feature of Oriental knowledge is that economy is considered a part of morality. Virtue leads to wealth, much like a healthy tree bears fruit. This is perhaps the best aspect of all of Yozan's reforms: his main goal was **to make his people *virtuous*.** He did not believe in wealth for its own sake, but, rather, **wealth was necessary to form a civilization.**

Some years after he took office, he reopened the clan-school. He named it Kojokwan, or the "Institute for the Promotion of Humility." One of the era's greatest scholars, Hosoi Heishu (Yozan's own tutor), was made the head master. The school provided many free scholarships to enable the poor to get a high-class education.

No good administration is complete without a way to heal the sick. Here too, Yozan had a solution. He started a medical school and opened a botanical garden to grow medicinal plants. He also

学の医者も育成した。つまり、ペリーが江戸湾に来航する50年前に、日本の山岳地方の一部で、すでに西洋医学が採用されていたのだ。

鷹山の社会改革のうち、2つのことに触れておきたい。彼は民の肉体的、また道徳的健康のために売春を禁じた。そして、伍什組合、つまり「5人と10人の組合」を設立した。次のように、鷹山自身の言葉で原則が述べられている。

伍什組合
それぞれ戸主のみ
を数える。

「 1. 五人組は、**家族のように**常に親しくし、それぞれの喜びと悲しみを分かち合わなければならない。

2. 十人組は、**親戚のように**しばしば行き来し、それぞれの家事に参加しなければならない。

3. 1つの村の者は、**友人のように**助け合い、互いに世話をしなければならない。

4. 五カ村組合の村は、**真の隣人のように**、困ったときに助け合わなければならない。

5. お互いに親切にするように。貧しい者、病人、もしくは身体が不自由な者は、五人組

trained several doctors in European medicine. So, fifty years before Perry landed in the Bay of Yedo, one of the mountain-districts of Japan had already adopted Western medicine.

I will mention two of Yozan's social reforms. He banned prostitution for the physical and moral health of his people, and he instituted *go-ju-kumiai*, or "the Associations of Five and Ten." Here are its principles, in Yozan's own words:

"I. Members of the Association of Five should always be in contact with each other and share the joys and sorrows of each, **as do members of a family**.

"II. Members of the Association of Ten should have frequent contact with each other, and participate in the affairs of each, **like blood relatives**.

"III. The people of a village should be **like friends** who help and serve one another.

"IV. The villages that make up the Association of Five Villages should help one another in times of trouble, **like true neighbors**.

"V. Be kind to each other. Let any poor, sick, or otherwise disabled person be cared for by

が世話をしなければならない。五人組に
その力がないときは、十人組が世話をし
なければならない。もし十人組の手に余
るときは、村が助けなければならない。も
し1つの村が災害に遭ってどうにもなら
ないときは、五カ村組合の4つの村が助け
なければならない。

6. 善を勧め、悪を戒め、皆が繁栄するよう助
けること——このために組合を作るので
ある。農地を放り出したり、ぜいたくにふ
けったりする者があれば、まず五人組が注
意し、つぎに十人組が注意しなければなら
ない。それでも行いを改めないなら、村役
人に報告し、しかるべき処分を受けさせな
ければならない。

享和2年（1802年）2月」

警察、説教師、学校、さまざまな「布告」によ
り、そして何よりも自身が良き手本となって、鷹
山は15万人の藩を理想の国に作り上げた。彼が
どれほど成功したかは、有名な学者、倉成竜渚に
よる次の記述で見ることができる。彼は「聖人
の治世」を見学するために米沢を訪れていた。

倉成竜渚
1748–1813、豊前
（大分県）生まれの
儒者。

his Association of Five. If the Association does not have the power to help, let his Association of Ten help. If his case is more than the latter can do for him, let his village help. If some disaster strikes one village so that it cannot help, then four of the Association of Five Villages should help.

"VI. To encourage the good, to teach the bad, and to help each person succeed—**this is why these associations are formed**. If a person neglects his farm, or indulges in luxuries, he should be warned first by his Association of Five, and then of Ten. If he does not change his ways, he must be reported to the village authority and receive due treatment.

February, 2nd year of Kyowa (1802)"

With his police, bishops, schools, various "instructions," and above all, with his own example, Yozan molded his clan of 150,000 people to his ideals. We can see how far he succeeded by the following account given by a well-known scholar, Kuranari Ryusho, who went to Yonezawa

「米沢には、『正札市』と呼ばれるものがある。道端に、ぞうり、果物、その他のものが置かれ、値段を付けて売られている。持ち主はいない。人々はそこへ行くと、正札どおりの金を置き、買った品物を取って通りすぎていく。この市場では誰も盗みをしないのだ。

鷹山の政府では、**もっとも地位の高い重臣が、もっとも貧乏である。**莅戸六郎兵衛は筆頭家老で、藩主にいちばん気に入られている家臣である。ところがその生活を見ると、食事も着物も貧しい学生を思わせるものだった」

莅戸六郎兵衛
1735–1804、米沢藩
上杉家の家臣。

これは、どこかのおとぎの国の話ではない。たった100年前に日本で、**実際にあったことなのである。**

to observe "how the saint rules his people."

"In Yonezawa there is something called the Label-Market. On the roadside, shoes, fruits and other items are put out for sale with their prices marked on them. Their owners are absent. People go there, leave the correct amount of money, take the purchased item, and pass on. Nobody steals at these markets.

"In Lord Yozan's government, **the highest officials are usually the poorest**. Nozoki Rokurobei is his prime minister, and he is the chief's favorite official. Yet, as I observed his ways of living, his food and clothing reminded me of those of a poor student."

These are not stories from some mythical land. **These were all realities** only a hundred years ago in Japan.

第6節

人となり

　我々の英雄を神のように崇めるなど、今日ではもう流行らない。だが鷹山に関しては、そのような危険はない。鷹山は、あらゆる人の中で類がないほど自分の欠点を知っていた。彼は**文字どおり**、じつに人間らしい人間だったのだ。

　たとえば、このような話がある。ある日、鷹山が師の講義を聞いていると、良い行いや奉仕をした家臣に褒美を与えるための名簿が渡された。鷹山はそれに目を通すと、講義が終わるまで脇へどけておいた。だが講義が終わったとき、その名簿のことを忘れてしまっていた。従者のひとりが、「**千乗の君**」として許されない不注意だと言って、彼を叱った。鷹山はひどく恥じ入り、座ったまま一夜を泣いて過ごした。翌朝も、「恥ずかしさのあまり朝食に手をつけられなかった」。師がやってきて、孔子の教えを引き合いに出して許したので、やっと食べることができたのである。

　鷹山の高潔さは、家庭や家族との関わりの中

千乗の君
乗は乗り物を数える単位。兵車を千台有するほどの大名の意味。

孔子
紀元前552–紀元前479、儒教の始祖。

VI.
The Man Himself

It is not fashionable these days to make gods out of our heroes. But there is no danger of this with Yozan. Of all men, Yozan was unique because he was aware of his own flaws. He was truly *human* **in the full sense of the term**.

Here's one story, for example: One day, while Yozan was listening to his teacher's lecture, he was given a list of his subjects who were to be rewarded for good deeds and services. Yozan looked at the list and put it away until the lecture was over. But when it ended, Yozan forgot about the list. One of his attendants scolded him for this carelessness that was unforgivable in a **"lord of thousands."** Yozan was so ashamed that he sat the whole night, weeping. The next morning, he "could not touch his breakfast because of his shame." He could only eat when his teacher came and forgave him, quoting a lesson from Confucius.

We can see Yozan's integrity most clearly in his

で、ひときわ明らかに見ることができる。彼が倹約家なのは述べたとおりだ——着物は質素で、少食だった。古い畳も、直せるものは替えなかった。破れた畳に自分で紙を貼って修理しているところを、よく見られたものだった。

彼は古いことわざを信じていた。「**自分を制することのできる者だけが、家庭を治めることができる。自分の家を整えることのできる者だけが、国を治めることができる**」。彼は優しい父親で、子どもたちの教育に熱心に取り組んだ。封建社会は世襲制なので、**民の将来の幸福は、息子たちがどのような統治者になるかにかかっている**。だから、息子たちに慈悲と犠牲の精神を教えた。彼が子どもたちに与えた教育の例として、孫娘に書いた多くの素晴らしい手紙のひとつが、ここにある。これは、いちばん年上の孫娘が、両親の屋敷を出て、町に住む夫のもとへ嫁ぐときに書いたものである。

「人が受けるもっとも大切な3つのものは、親、師、君主の恩である……。命があるのは親のおかげだ。自分の体は親の一部であることを忘れてはならない。だから親に仕えるときは、いつも誠実に、そして正直にふるまいなさい。こうすれば、たとえ過ちがあっても、良い行いからそれほ

鷹山の妻子
正妻の幸姫には知的障害があり、30歳で亡くなり、子はなかった。側室のお豊の方とは二子をもうけたがどちらも早く亡くなり、鷹山の血筋は残らなかった。

三姫
上杉治広（鷹山の養嗣子《家督相続人》）の長女。

home and domestic relations. We know he was frugal—he wore simple clothing and ate little. He never replaced his old *tatami* if he could fix it. He was often seen patching up torn mats by pasting papers over them.

He believed in the old saying, "**A man rules his family only if he can rule himself**. Only a man whose house is in order can rule a nation." He was a kind father who made great efforts to educate his children. He understood that in the hereditary system of feudalism, **his people's future happiness depended on the kind of rulers his sons would be**. So, he taught his boys charity and sacrifice. Here, as an example of how he educated his children, is one of many beautiful letters he wrote to his granddaughters. It was written to his eldest granddaughter when she was leaving her parents' mansion to join her husband in the city.

"A person's three most important influences are his parents, his teacher, and his master. . . . We owe our lives to our parents. Never forget that your body is a part of theirs. So, in service to them, always act sincerely and honestly. This way, even if you make mistakes, you are never far from doing

ど離れることはない……。領地を治めることは、とても手に負えないように思うかもしれない。しかし、領地の『もと』は整った家庭である。そして、妻と夫の間に正しい関係がなければ、整った家庭は作れない……。あなたは若い女だから、美しく着飾りたいと思うのは無理もないだろう。だが、これまで教わってきた倹約の習慣を忘れてはならない。養蚕や、女としての他の仕事に励みなさい。それと同時に、美しい和歌で心を養いなさい。ただ楽しむことだけを求めてはいけない。あらゆる学問の目的は、徳を身につけることだからだ。それゆえ、善を行い、悪を避けるよう教えてくれるものを学びなさい……。あなたの夫は父として民を導かなければならず、あなたは母として民を愛さなければならない。そうすれば、民はあなたたちを親として敬う。これ以上の喜びがあるだろうか」

この勤勉な男は70年の人生を送った。彼は自分の望みと目的のほとんどを達成した。藩を安定させ、民を豊かにし、全領地をよみがえらせた。そうして、鷹山は安らかに人生を終えた。文政5年（1822年）3月19日、彼は世を去った。鷹山の死について、このように書かれている。「民は、自分の祖父母が亡くなったかのように泣い

「為せば成る　為さねば成らぬ何事も　成らぬは人の　為さぬなりけり」
鷹山が家臣に教訓として詠み、今に伝わる名句。

good. . . . You may think ruling a dominion is an impossible task. But know that the 'root' of a dominion is its orderly families. And there can be no orderly families without the right relationship between wife and husband. . . . Because you are a young woman, it is natural that you will want to dress nicely. But don't forget the frugal habits that you have been taught. Devote yourself to silk-worm raising and other womanly work. At the same time, feed your mind with beautiful poetry. Do not simply seek entertainment, for the purpose of all knowledge is to lead us to virtue. Therefore, learn things that will teach you to do good and avoid evil. . . . Your husband should teach the people as their father, and you should love them as their mother. Then they honor you both as their parents. What joy is better than this?"

This hard-working man lived for seventy years. He achieved most of his hopes and goals: he firmly established his clan, supplied his people well, and revived his whole territory. And so, Yozan ended his life in peace. On March 19th of the 5th year of Bunsei (1822), he passed away. This is what was written about his death: "The people wept as

た。その悲しみは筆舌に尽くしがたい。葬儀の日には、何万人もの会葬者が道にあふれた。頭をたれ、涙を流して、むせび泣いた。山、川、草木さえも、ともに嘆き悲しんだ」

if they had lost their grandparents. No pen could describe their sadness. On the day of his funeral, tens of thousands of mourners filled the roads. With heads bowed, they wailed and wept. Even the mountains, rivers, and plants joined in sorrow."

二宮尊徳

農民聖者

Chapter 3

NINOMIYA SONTOK

A Peasant Saint

19世紀初頭の日本の農業

日本には海岸があり、貿易上の利点もたくさんあるが、それでも国民の生活は主に農業に支えられている。しかし、耕作に適しているのは国土の20％のみである。だから土地から最大の収穫を得るために、創造力を用い、勤勉に働かなければならない。

日本の農業は、世界でもっとも目覚ましいものだと思う。いかに狭い土地も、いかに小さな植物も、ほとんど親の愛情のような心づかいと世話を受ける。その結果、完璧なまでに栽培された1300万エーカーの農地を持つようになったのだ。

1エーカー
およそ4047平方
メートル、1200坪。

江戸時代
1603-1868、徳川幕
府の政局安定作に
より長期安定政権
が確立し、長期の
平和状態を日本に
もたらした。

しかし19世紀の初めには、日本の農業は悲惨な状態だった。泰平の世が200年も続いたため、あらゆる階級の者が怠け、しかもぜいたくになった。これが、たちまち農地に影響した。多くの地方で、土地から得られる収入が3分の2も減少した。**かつて実り豊かだった農地は荒れ果てた。**ようやく育ったわずかな作物も年貢に取られてし

I.
Japanese Agriculture in the Beginning of the Nineteenth Century

Despite all of Japan's seacoasts and commercial advantages, the main livelihood of our people comes from farming. However, only 20 percent of our land is cultivable. So we must be creative and hardworking to maximize production from our land.

We consider **Japanese agriculture to be the most remarkable in the world**. Every bit of land and every little plant is given so much care and attention that it almost borders parental affection. As a result, we have 13,000,000 acres of farmed land that are tended to perfection.

But, in the beginning of the nineteenth century, Japanese agriculture was in a terrible state. With two hundred years of continued peace, all classes became lazy, as well as luxurious. This immediately affected our fields. In many places, the revenue from land decreased by two-thirds. Our **once-productive fields went wild**. What little could be

まう。まともに働かないので、村は貧しくなり、人々はだましあうようになる。こうして道徳が失われたので、自然は民に報酬を与えることを拒んだ。そのとき、**自然の法を理解し、それに従う精神を持つ1人の男が生まれたのである。**

grown was taken as feudal dues. Without honest work, villages fell into poverty and men took up dishonest ways. And without good morals, Nature refused to reward her people. Then a man was born **whose spirit understood and obeyed Nature's laws.**

少年時代

二宮金次郎
1787-1856、相模国
（現在の神奈川県）
出身の農政家、思
想家。

　尊徳（徳を尊ぶ人）とも呼ばれる二宮金次郎
は、天明7年（1787年）に生まれた。父は相模の
国にある小村の貧しい農夫だった。尊徳が16歳
のときに父が亡くなり、尊徳と2人の弟は親戚に
引き取られた。

『大学』
儒教の経典のひと
つ。

　尊徳は伯父の家に引き取られたが、できるだ
け面倒をかけないように努めた。毎日夜中まで
懸命に働いた。しかし、**無学な大人になってはい
けない**と思い、孔子の『大学』を読み始めた。毎
日、一日中働いた後で、尊徳はこの本で勉強し
た。だがすぐに、読書しているところを伯父に見
つかり、灯りの油を無駄に使ったと叱られた。そ
こで尊徳は、自分の油を手に入れて灯りをとも
せるようになるまでは、勉強をあきらめること
にした。

　翌春、尊徳は小さな土地を耕し、アブラナの
種を植えた。休みの日をすべて使って、この作物
の世話をした。すると年の終わりに、大きな袋に

II.
Boyhood

Ninomiya Kinjiro, nicknamed Sontok (Admirer of Virtue), was born in the seventh year of Tenmei (1787). His father was a poor farmer in a tiny village in Sagami province. He died when Sontok was 16 years old, and Sontok and his two little brothers were sent to relatives.

Sontok went to live with one of his uncles, where he tried to be as little trouble as possible. He worked hard until midnight every day. But, he felt **he should not grow up illiterate**, so he began reading Confucius' *Great Learning*. Every day, after a full day of work, Sontok studied this book. But soon his uncle found him studying and scolded him for wasting his oil. So, Sontok gave up studying until he could have oil of his own to burn.

Next spring, Sontok worked a little piece of land and planted some rape-seed. He spent all his holidays taking care of this crop. At year's end, he

いっぱいの菜種が取れた。彼はこれを自分の手で作ったのだ——自然が、彼の勤勉な労働に対して褒美をくれたのである。彼は菜種を油に変えた。もう伯父から油をもらわなくていいと思うとうれしくてたまらない。喜び勇んで、勉強を再開した。ところが、そうはいかなかった！ 伯父は怒った。**自分の働き手に、そんな儲からないことで時間を無駄にさせる余裕はない**と言うのだ。そして再び、尊徳は伯父の言葉に従い、読書のかわりに、むしろ編みやわらじ作りにいそしむようになった。

　休みの日に、尊徳は作物で実験をした。アブラナがよく育ったので、次は米で試してみた。小さな沼を見つけ、水をくみだし、他の農夫たちが捨てた苗を植えた。そして秋には、1俵（約70リットル）の米を手にした。**自分のささやかな努力で、これほど多くの米を産み出せた**のを見て、彼はとても喜んだ。このようにして尊徳は、**懸命に働いて自然の法に従う者には、自然が誠実に報いてくれる**ことを学んだのである。

　数年後、尊徳は伯父の家を出て、父の粗末な家に戻った。何年も見捨てられていたため、土地は荒れ果てていた。だが尊徳は辛抱強く、勇んで働いた。まもなく、どの土地にも作物が実るように

had a large bagful of the seed. He had produced this on his own—Nature had rewarded him for his hard work. He turned the seed into oil, and he was glad that he wouldn't have to take from his uncle. Happily, he began his lessons again. But no! The uncle was angry. **He could not afford to let one of his workers waste time on something so unprofitable**, he said. Again, Sontok followed his uncle's advice and began to work at weaving and sandal-making instead of reading.

On his holidays, Sontok experimented with crops. His rape-seed crop had grown well, and next he tried rice. He found a little pond, drained it, and planted rice from the seedlings that other farmers had thrown away. By autumn, he had a bagful (about 70 liters) of grain. He was overjoyed to see that **his own humble effort could yield so much**. This is how he learned that **Nature is faithful to those who work hard and obey her laws**.

A few years later, Sontok left his uncle's house and returned to his father's cottage. Abandoned for many years, the land had grown wild. But Sontok was patient and willing to work. Soon, every bit of

なった。何年もたたないうちに、良い暮しができるようになり、その倹約と勤勉さのゆえに人々に尊敬されるようになった。彼はこれらすべてを自分の力でやり遂げた。そして、彼に倣おうとする人には喜んで力を貸した。

his land was producing again. Before long, he made a comfortable life and became well respected for his economy and hard work. He had done all this for himself, and he was ready to help others do so too.

第3節

能力の試練

大久保忠真
1778–1837、小田原
藩第7代藩主。

尊徳はまもなく小田原藩主の目に留まった。藩主は、尊徳のような男は貴重な人材であり、もっと役に立つ事業に使えるはずだと気づいたのである。

下野の国
現在の栃木県。大久保家の分家である宇津家の知行地があった。

小田原藩主の領地には、下野の国に、物井、横田、東沼という3つの村があった。これらの村は、数世代にわたって放置されていたため、貧困に陥り、犯罪がはびこっていた。村にはかつて450軒の農家があり、毎年1万俵の年貢を産み出していた。ところが今では、人口は以前のわずか3分の1であり、貧しさにあえぐ農民は、よくても2千俵しか産出できない。**貧困によって道徳がすたれ**、村には賭博者が群がっていた。

小田原藩主には、ある考えがあった。これらの村にもとの豊かさと生産性を取り戻すことができる者なら、すべての同じような村（そういう村がたくさんあった）の回復を委ねることができ

III.
The Test of His Ability

Sontok soon caught the attention of the Lord of Odawara. The lord knew that a man like Sontok was a valuable asset, and that he could be used for greater good.

The Lord of Odawara's territory included the three villages of Monoi, Yokota, and Tosho in the province of Shimotsuke. These villages had fallen into poverty and sin after several generations of neglect. The villages once had 450 families who produced feudal dues of 10,000 bags of rice every year. But now, the population was only one-third of what it had been, and the impoverished farmers could only produce 2,000 bags of rice at most. **With poverty came lack of morals**, and the villages were overrun with gamblers.

The Lord of Odawara had an idea. A man who could bring these villages back to their original wealth and productivity could be entrusted to restore *all* such villages (of which there were many).

る。また、そういう人物なら、村人に尊敬され、地位の高い者たちから批判される恐れもなく統治者となることができる。

これが、藩主が尊徳に頼んだ仕事だった。しかし農民である尊徳は、そのような仕事をするには身分が低すぎると言って断った。「私はただの貧しい百姓です。この人生で成し遂げられそうなのは、せいぜい我が家の財産をよみがえらせることくらいです」と言った。**3年の長きにわたって、藩主は尊徳にこの仕事を引き受けるよう頼み続けた**。そして、ついに尊徳は断りきれなくなり、可能な解決法を考えるため3つの村を訪れた。

尊徳は村に数か月間滞在し、村人とともに過ごした。土壌、森、水路のようす、他にも多くのことを調べた。そして必要な情報がすべて集まると、藩主に報告した。

「この貧しい民に平和と富を取り戻すことができるのは、『仁愛の術（仁術）』だけです」と彼は言った。「金は彼らの助けにならないでしょう。というより、金を与えるのをやめるべきです。金は**民の間に、貪欲や、怠惰や、争いをもたらす**からです。荒れ地は自らの資源で改良しなければならず、貧しい者は自らの力で立ち直らなければなりません。もし農地から2俵の米が収穫でき

仁術
儒教の最高の徳である仁徳（思いやり、慈しみ）を行う方法。

Such a man could earn the respect of the villagers and become a governor without fear of criticism from the higher classes.

This was the job the lord offered Sontok. But the peasant declined, saying his background was too humble for such work. "I am just a poor farmer," he said. "All I can expect to accomplish in my life is to restore my own family property." **For three long years the lord asked Sontok to take on this work.** Finally, when Sontok could not say no any longer, he visited the three villages to think of possible solutions.

Sontok stayed in the villages for months, living among the people. He studied the soil, the forests, the water supply, and more. When he finally had all the information he needed, he reported to his lord.

"Only the 'art of love' (仁術) can restore peace and wealth to these poor people," he said. "Money will not help them. In fact, we should stop giving them money, because it **leads to greed, laziness, and arguments among the people**. The wilderness must be improved by its own resources, and the poor must help themselves. If a field can produce two bags of rice, one bag should go to feed the people, and the

たら、1俵は民の食料とし、もう1俵は村の発展のために使うべきです。**仁愛、勤勉、自助の精神**を用いるなら、約10年後には、これらの村を再び豊かにすることができると思います」。藩主はこの計画に満足した。それは、道徳を経済計画の要とするものだった。

尊徳は政策も条例も作らなかった。**誠実に働けば、ほぼどんなことでも成し遂げられる**という、純粋な信念だけがあった。だから、あらゆるぜいたくを避け、質素な着物を着、1日2時間しか眠らなかった。どの使用人よりも早く畑に出て、皆が帰るまで残った。

尊徳にとって最高の働き手とは、もっとも多く働けるものではなく、**もっともよい動機で働く者**だった。たとえば、彼の働き手のなかに、もう若者ほどの力がない年老いた男がいた。彼はいつも切り株を掘り起こしていた。それは退屈で、なかなかはかどらず、難しい仕事──つまり、誰もやりたがらない仕事だった。でもその男は、他の者が休んでいるときでさえ、いつも切り株を掘り起こしていた。皆は彼のことを「根っこ掘り」と呼び、ほとんど気にもかけなかった。しかし、尊徳はしっかりと目を注いでいた。

賃金を支払う日になり、全員が集まった。いち

other should fund the villages' development. If we use **love, hard work, and self-reliance**, I think we can bring these villages back to wealth in about ten years." The lord was happy with this plan, which made *morals* an essential part of economic reform.

Sontok had no policies or regulations. He just had a simple belief that **sincere work could accomplish almost anything**. So, he avoided all luxuries, put on simple clothes, and slept only two hours a day. He was in the field before any of his men and remained there until everyone had left.

For Sontok, the best worker was not the man who could do the most work, but **the man who worked with the best motive**. One of his workers, for example, was an elderly man who was not as strong as the young. He was always working on stumps. It is a boring, slow, and difficult job—a job nobody wanted to do. But he always worked at these stumps, even when the others were resting. They called him "Stump-digger" and paid little attention to him. But Sontok was watching.

On pay-day, everybody gathered. The most

最高額の賃金
「根っこ掘り」には
当時の労働者の年
俸に相当する額で
ある15両の褒賞
が与えられた。

ばん価値のある仕事をした者に、いちばん多くの金が与えられる。皆が驚いたことに、最高額の賃金を与える者として、尊徳は「根っこ掘り」の名を呼んだ。根っこ掘り本人でさえ驚いた。「私は1人分の賃金をもらう値打ちもありません」と彼は言った。「年寄りで、他の者たちのような力もありません。先生はきっとお間違えになったのです。どうか、このお金を返させてください」

「いいや」と尊徳は答えた。「おまえは、他の誰もがやりたがらない仕事をやった。そして誰にも気づかれず、ほめられなくても気にしなかった。**村のために本当に役立つことをしたかっただけだ。**おまえが切り株をすべて取り除いてくれたから、私たちの仕事はやりやすくなったのだ。この金はおまえの誠実さへの褒美だ。受け取りなさい。このような誠実さを目にすることほど、うれしいことはない」

男は子どものように泣きだし、村じゅうの者が感動した。

もちろん、尊徳やそのやり方に反対する者も大勢いた。だが尊徳は、反対派にも同じく「仁術」で打ち勝った。数年後、3つの村は豊かな実りをもたらすようになった。しかし、尊徳は、**10年間の飢饉に耐えられるだけの十分な蓄えがなけれ**

money was given to the workers who had done the most valuable work. To everyone's surprise, Sontok called up the "stump-digger" for the highest pay. Even the stump-digger was shocked. "I am not worthy of even one man's pay," he said. "I am old and not as strong as the others. Your lordship must be mistaken. Please, take back this gold."

"No," replied Sontok. "You did the work that nobody else wanted to do. You didn't care that nobody noticed or gave you credit. **You only wanted to provide a real service to our villages**. Our work was made easier because you cleared all the stumps. The gold rewards your honesty. Accept it. Nothing makes me happier than seeing such honesty as yours."

The man wept like a child, and the whole village was impressed.

Of course, many people opposed Sontok and his ways, but he won them over by similar "arts of love." After several years, the three villages became productive. But Sontok believed that **no district was healthy until it had enough resources to last**

9年の蓄え
前漢時代の中国の経書である『礼記』の「王制篇」に「國無九年之蓄。日不足。無六年之蓄。日急。無三年之蓄。日國非其國也」とある。

ば、どの地域も健全とはいえないと信じていた。中国の思想家の「9年の蓄えがない国は危ない。3年の蓄えがない国は、もはや国とはいえない」という言葉に従ったのである。この見方によれば、今日の裕福な大国でさえ「もはや国とはいえない」だろう。

　約束の10年の終わりには、日本でもっとも貧しかった土地が、国でもっとも整い、もっとも恵まれ、そしてもっとも肥沃な地域になった。村々は以前のように1万俵の米を生産するだけでなく、今では数棟の倉庫を持ち、そこには何年も持ちこたえられるほどの米がぎっしり詰まっていた。尊徳は有名になり、国じゅうの地位の高い人々から、村の再興法について指導を求められた。彼の助言はいつもじつに単純で、金がかからず、誠実だった。尊徳が勤勉と自助を一心に求めたことは、当時の社会に大きな感銘を与えた。

ten years of scarcity. He followed the words of a Chinese philosopher who said, "A country without nine years' resources is in danger. One without three years' is not a country at all." According to this view, even the wealthiest of nations today is "not a nation at all."

At the end of the promised ten years, the poorest land in the empire had become the most orderly, best supplied, and most fertile district in the country. Not only did the villages produce 10,000 bags of rice as before, but they now had several warehouses filled with enough rice to last for years. Sontok became famous, and nobles from all parts of the country asked for his instructions on how to restore villages. His advice was always so simple, so cheap, and so sincere. Sontok's devotion to hard work and self-reliance left a great impression on communities of his time.

第4節

個人的援助

　尊徳が、**苦しんでいる友に与えた援助**について、少し話しておきたい。彼はまったく独立独行の人で、誠実さと勤勉によって解決できない問題はないと信じていた。

　ある日、村の名主が尊徳のところへ助言を求めてやってきた。名主は村人たちから尊敬されず、忠義も尽くしてもらえないので、尊徳にその理由を尋ねた。

　「それは、**自分ばかり大切にしている**からだ」尊徳は答えた。「自分のものをすべて与えたら、村人から敬われるだろう」

　「どうやったら、そんなことができるのですか？」と名主は聞いた。

　「土地も、家も、着物も、何もかも売りなさい」尊徳は答えた。「それで得た金をすべて村の資金にし、**自分のすべてを皆への奉仕に捧げなさい**」

　名主は2、3日よく考えさせてほしいと言った。ようやく、自分には犠牲が大きすぎるという結論

IV.

Individual Services

Let me talk briefly about **the help Sontok gave his suffering friends**. He was a completely self-made man, and he believed there was no problem that couldn't be solved by sincerity and hard work.

One day, a mayor of a village came to Sontok for advice. He had lost the respect and loyalty of his people and he asked Sontok why.

"Because **you only love yourself**," Sontok replied. "People will only respect you if you give them your all."

"How can I do that?" asked the mayor.

"Sell your land, your house, your clothes, everything," Sontok replied. "Whatever money you make by selling your things, give to the village fund, and **give yourself completely to public service**."

The mayor asked for several days to think it over. Finally, he decided that the sacrifice was too much

が出た。尊徳は言った。「自分の家族の面倒が見られないと心配しているのだな。だが、**おまえが自分の役目を果たすなら、私も助言者として自分の役目を果たそう**」

　名主は彼の助言に従った。すると、たちまち村人から尊敬されるようになった。名主が貧しい生活を送っている間、尊徳は自分の食料や日用品を与えて彼を支えた。だがまもなく、村じゅうの人が名主を援助するようになり、しばらくすると、名主は以前より裕福になったのだ。

　尊徳と近づきになるのは容易なことではなかった。彼はとても忙しかったので、見知らぬ人が助けを求めてやってきても、断わることが多かった。もっとも忍耐強い人だけが、なんとか彼に会うことができた。かつてある仏僧がいて、檀家のひとりのことで助言を得ようと長い距離を歩いてきたが、やはり断られた。僧は待つことに決め、昼夜を問わず何日も、師の家の前に座り続けたので、やっと中へ招かれて会うことができた。だが、その後何年にもわたって、尊徳の金と助言と友情を受けることになったのである。尊徳と親しくなることは難しかったが、いったんそうなると、彼は友情を惜しむことがなかった。

for him. Sontok said, "You are afraid that you won't be able to care for your own family. But **if *you* do *your* part, I, as your adviser, will also do *my* part.**"

The mayor followed his advice, and he immediately gained the respect of the people. While the mayor lived in poverty, Sontok supported him with his own food and supplies. But soon the whole village came to the mayor's support, and in a short time, he was wealthier than before.

Sontok was not an easy man to approach. He was very busy, and strangers who came to him for help were often turned away. Only the most persistent people could arrange a meeting with him. There was once a Buddhist priest, who walked a long distance to get advice for one of his parishioners, but he was turned away. He decided to wait and sat patiently for many days and nights in front of the teacher's house before he was invited in for a meeting. However, this priest would receive much of Sontok's gold, advice, and friendship over the years. Although it was difficult to get Sontok's friendship, he was generous with it once he gave it.

公共事業

やがて尊徳は、さらに多くの公共事業を手がけるようになっていった。生涯の間に、広大な領地を持つ藩主のうち少なくとも10人の手助けをした。晩年には、その働きがひじょうに掛け替えのないものとなり、幕府にも用いられるようになった。

当然のことながら、主人である小田原藩主がいちばん多く彼の力を借りた。**もっとも重要な貢献のひとつは、1836年の大飢饉のときのものだった。**何千人もの人々が餓死寸前となり、助けるよう命じられたのだ。彼は小田原に駆けつけると、飢えている民に食料を与えるため、穀物倉の鍵を渡すよう役人たちに頼んだ。「主君の直筆の許可状が届くまでは渡せない」というのが役人の返答だった。「よろしい」尊徳は応じた。「だが、直筆の許可状が届くのを待つ間に、さらに多くの民が飢え死にするだろうから、私たちも食べるべきではない。**使者が戻るまでの4日間、断食することにしよう。**そうすれば民の苦しみがわ

天保の大飢饉
1833–1839、大雨洪水と冷害による大凶作。各地で餓死者を出し、米価が急騰し、百姓一揆や乱の原因となった。

V.

Public Services

Sontok went on to provide many more public services. During his lifetime, he helped at least ten lords representing large territories. Near the end of his life his service became so invaluable that he was hired by the Central Government.

Naturally, his own Lord of Odawara received the most help from him. **One of his most important services was during the great famine of 1836**. Thousands of people were starving to death, and he was ordered to help. He rushed to Odawara and asked the officials there to give him the key to the granary so he could feed the starving people. "Not until we have the lord's written permission," was their answer. "All right," Sontok replied. "But, since many more people will die of starvation while we wait for written permission, we should not eat either. **Let's fast for four days until your messenger returns**. Then we may learn what the

かるかもしれない」。4日間も食べずに過ごすことを考えただけで、役人たちはぞっとした。そしてすぐに鍵を尊徳に渡したので、民は食料を与えられた。人々を管理するすべての者が、無用で形式的な手続きを待っている間に、このことを思い出してくれさえしたらいいのだが！

このとき、尊徳は「飢饉からの救済法」として有名な演説をした。ここに引用してみよう。

「作物が不作で民が飢えるなら、それは治める者以外のだれの責任か？ 治める者は、民の世話をするよう任されている。民を導き、平和に暮らせるようにするのが義務である。これをするために多くの禄をもらっているのだ。ところが今、民が飢えているというのに責任を取っていない。これほどの悪を私は知らない。治める者は解決策を考え出さなければならない。もしできないなら、自分が飢え死にするべきだ！ そして役人たちも全員、食べるのをやめて死ぬべきだ。彼らも自分の義務を怠り、民を苦しめたからだ。

こうすれば、飢えている民にすぐ効果が現れる。民は、『ご家老とお役人が、私たちの飢えのせいで責めを負われた。でもこれは私たちの責任だ。私たちが怠けたのだ。お役人が私たちのため

people are suffering." The officers were horrified by the thought of not eating for four days. They immediately gave him the key and the people were fed. If only *all* guardians of the people would remember this while waiting for useless formalities!

At this time, Sontok gave his famous talk on "How to Deliver Relief from Famine." Here is an excerpt:

"When the crops fail and the people starve, whose fault is it but the ruler's? He is trusted to care for the people. It is his duty to lead them and enable them to live in peace. He is paid well for this service. But now that his people are starving, he does not take responsibility for it. I don't know anything worse than this. He needs to come up with a solution, and if not, he should starve himself and *die*! Then all of his officers should also stop eating and *die*, because they have also neglected their duty and made the people suffer.

"This will have an immediate effect on the starving people. They will say, 'The governor and his officers blamed themselves for our hunger, but it is our fault. We were lazy. Our officers died for

に死んだのだから、私たちが今飢えて死ぬのは当然だ』と言うだろう。このようにして民はもはや飢えも死も恐れなくなり、金持ちは貧しい者に富を分け与えるだろう。だから**指導者をまず餓死させよ、そうすれば民は救われるだろう**」

　もちろん尊徳の助力により、そのような極端な手段は必要なかった。農民たちには穀物と金が貸し付けられた。そして倹約と勤勉の指導のもと、自分たちが食べ、借金を返済するのに十分な作物を作ることができたのである。

　大小にかかわらず、どのような事業でも、尊徳のやり方は単純だった。まず、1つの村——たいていはその地方でもっとも貧しい村——に専念し、自分の方針に従って村を変える。これがいつも、いちばん難しいところだった。しかし**1つの村が救われると、その地方全体を変えはじめる土台となった**。尊徳から学んだ農民たちは、自分たちが師に助けてもらったように、近隣の人々を助けるよう求められる。この良い手本を目にし、同じような困難を生き抜いた人々が喜んで助けてくれるので、地方全体がついには尊徳の教えに従うようになるのだった。

　「1つの村を救える方法は、国全体を救うことができる。**原理はまったく同じなのだ**」尊徳はよ

us, and it is proper for us to now die of hunger.' In this way, they are no longer afraid of hunger and death, and the rich may share his wealth with the poor. Therefore, **let the leaders die first from fasting, and the people will be saved**."

Of course, with Sontok's help, such drastic measures were not necessary. The farmers were loaned grain and money. Under instructions of frugality and hard work, they were able to produce enough crops to eat and pay back their loans.

The way Sontok worked on any project, large or small, was simple. First, he concentrated on one village—usually the poorest in the district— and converted it to his ways. This was usually the hardest part. But, **with one village rescued, he had a base to start converting the whole district**. The peasants who learned from him were required to help their neighbors, just as they were helped by their teacher. With this good example, and with help freely given by men who had lived through similar difficulties, the whole district would eventually adopt his teachings.

"The method that can rescue a village can rescue the whole country; **the principle is just the same**,"

くこう言ったものである。「この1つの仕事に専念しよう。そうすれば手本となって、国全体を救えるだろう」

　もちろん尊徳は、人生の最期まで勤勉な働き者だった。今日でも、この人物の教えに忠実な農民団体が、日本のさまざまな地域に散在しており、彼の知恵を貧しい人々に広げようと努めている。

Sontok used to say. "Let's devote ourselves to this one piece of work, and our example may save the whole nation."

Naturally he was a hard-working man until the end of his life. Today, scattered through different parts of the country are societies of farmers who are loyal to the teachings of this man, and they work to spread his wisdom to the needy.

中江 藤樹
村の先生

Chapter 4
NAKAE TOJU
A Village Teacher

第1節

昔の日本の教育

西洋人によく尋ねられる質問がある。「私たちが救いに行く前、日本ではどのような教育をしていたのですか？　あなたたち日本人は、**異教徒のなかではとりわけ賢い人々**のようです。なんらかの訓練をしているにちがいありません」

私たちの答えは、たいてい次のようなものである。

「そうです。私たちはひじょうに多くの教育を受けました。モーセの十戒のうち少なくとも8つは、幼い頃に学びます。暴力は良くないこと、天地は利己的な者を助けてくれないこと、財産だけを目的としてはいけないこと、その他たくさんのことを知っています。学校もあり、教師もいましたが、西洋で見るものとはかなり違います。何よりもまず、**学校を、職業を学ぶ場とは考えませんでした**。私たちは『真の人間』——君子——英語で言う『ジェントルマン』のような人間になるために、そこへ送られたのです。また、多くのさまざまな教科を一度に教えられることもあり

モーセの十戒
旧約聖書の出エジプト記に登場する、モーセが神から与えられた戒律。

I.

Education in Old Japan

Many Westerners ask us, "What kind of education did you have in Japan before we Westerners came to save you? You Japanese seem to be **the cleverest group of people among heathens**. You must have had some training."

Our answer is usually the following:

"Yes, we've had quite a lot of education. We learn at least eight out of the Ten Commandments while we are very young. We know that violence is wrong, the universe does not help the selfish, that property should not be our sole aim, and many other things. We had schools too and teachers, quite different from what we see in the West. First of all, **we never thought of schools as places to learn a profession**. We were sent there to become 'true men'—*kunshi*—which is like "gentlemen" in English. We were not taught a dozen different subjects at the same time. Our old teachers thought that we must

ませんでした。日本の昔の教師は、全種類の知識を数年で詰めこむべきではないと考えていたのです。歴史、詩、作法についてもたくさん教わりましたが、**おもに道徳について、しかも実際的な道徳のみ**教わりました。宗教は、学校では決して教えません。宗教を学ぶためには寺へ行きましたから、他の地でよく見られるように、学校で宗教的な議論をすることはありませんでした。

　また、クラスに分かれて教わるのではなく、**能力のちがう者がすべて一緒に集められました。**人はそれぞれ違うので、顔と顔を合わせ、魂と魂で向き合って、個人的に扱われるべきだと教師は信じていました。ですから、1人ずつ教えられたのです。適者生存に基づいた教育制度では、君子を育てる効果はないと考えられていました。このように日本の昔の教師は、教育理論においてソクラテスやプラトンと同じ意見だったのです。

　このことはまた、教師と生徒の関係がとても近いということも意味していました。私たちは教師のことを**先生、つまり『先に生まれた人』**と呼びました。これは、私たちより先に真理を理解するようになったということを表しています。教師はひじょうに尊敬され、その尊敬は、親や藩主に見せるものと変わらないほどでした。さら

ソクラテス
紀元前469頃–紀元前399、古代ギリシアの教育者、哲学者。

プラトン
紀元前427–紀元前347、古代ギリシアの哲学者。ソクラテスの弟子で、アリストテレスの師。

not be crammed with all kinds of knowledge in a few years. We were taught much History, Poetry, and Manners; but **mainly Morals, and only of the practical kind**. Theology was never taught in our schools. We had temples to go to for that, and our schools never had the religious arguments often seen in other lands.

"Also, we were not taught in classes, **with all different abilities grouped together**. Our teachers believed that people are individual, and that we must be dealt with personally, face to face and soul to soul. So they taught us one by one. The system of education based on the survival of the fittest was considered ineffective for making *kunshi*. In this way, our old-time teachers agreed with Socrates and Plato in their theory of education.

"This also meant that teacher-student relationships were very close. We called our teachers *sensei*, or 'men born before'. This referred to how they had come to understand the truth before us. They deserved the highest respect, similar to the respect we show to our parents and feudal lords. Indeed, *sensei*, parents, and *kimi* (lord) constituted

にいえば、先生、親、君（藩主）を三位一体として、私たちは崇拝したのです。日本の若者にとっていちばん困る問題は、その3人が同時に溺れていて、1人しか救えないとき、誰を救うかというものでした。ですから、弟子（生徒）にとって最高の徳とは、自分の先生（師）のために命を捨てることと考えられていたのです。しかし今日、近代の教育制度のもとでは、教授のために命を捨てる学生の話など聞いたことがありません」

　私たちがこのように答えても、**西洋の友人たちはたいてい褒めてはくれない**。だからこのエッセイのなかで、日本でもっとも偉大な先生のひとりとみなされている人物の考えについて、語っておきたい。そうすれば、西洋の友人たちも、私たちのことをもっと理解してくれるだろう。

the trinity of our worship. The most troubling question for Japanese youth was which he would save if the three of them were drowning at the same time, and he could only save one. It was considered, therefore, the highest virtue for *deshi* (disciples) to lay down their lives for their *sensei* (master). However, we've never heard of students today dying for their professor in our modern system of education."

When we give this answer, **our Western friends usually do not applaud**. So, in this essay I'd like to share the ideas of a man whom we consider one of our greatest *sensei*, so that our friends in the West may understand us better.

第2節

青年時代

西暦1608年当時、男たちの主な仕事は戦うことだった。**哲学や学問は、現実的な男たちにとって役に立たないものと思われていた。**そのようなときに、日本でもっとも進歩的な思想家のひとりが、近江の国で生まれたのである。

ほとんど四国の祖父母のもとで育った藤樹は、幼い頃から感受性の鋭い子どもだった。侍の息子なので、主に武芸を学んでいた。しかし11歳のとき、孔子の『大学』の重要な一節を読み、それが彼の将来の進路を変えることになった。そこにはこう書かれていた。「天子からごくふつうの庶民にいたるまで、**人の主な目的は、生活を正しく整えることにある**」。この考えに、若い藤樹の心は驚きに満たされた。そして、生活を整えること、つまり、できるだけ完璧な人間になることを人生の目的にしようと決心した。

17歳のとき、孔子の『四書』一式を手に入れることができた。彼は空いた時間をすべて読書

中江藤樹
1608-1648、近江国
（滋賀県）出身の、
陽明学者。

『大学』
儒教の経典のひと
つ。

『四書』
儒教の経書である
『大学』、『中庸』、
『論語』、『孟子』の
総称。

II.

Early Years

In the year 1608 of the Christian era, the main business of men was to fight. **Philosophy and learning was considered useless to practical men**. At such a time, one of Japan's most advanced thinkers was born in the province of Omi.

Brought up mostly by his grandparents in the island of Shikoku, Toju showed sensitivity at an early age. As the son of a samurai, he trained mostly in the art of war. But he was eleven years old when he read an important passage in Confucius' *Great Learning* that was to change the future of his career. He read: "From the Emperor down to the most common people, **man's chief aim is in the right ordering of his life**." This idea filled young Toju with wonder. He decided that his life goal would be to order his life, or to become as a perfect a man as possible.

When he was seventeen, he was able to get a complete set of Confucius' *Four Books*. He spent

にあてた。しかし当時、侍の主な仕事は戦うことだったので、藤樹は夜にだけ隠れて勉強しなければならなかった。ところが彼の秘密が見つかってしまった。ある日、友人のひとりが夜中の勉強のことをからかって、彼を「孔子さま」と呼んだ。「このばか者！」と若き藤樹は答えた。「私を孔子さまと呼んだりして、聖人を侮辱するな。私の学問好きをからかうとは悲しいことだ。あわれな奴め！　侍の仕事は戦いだけではなく、平和なときの仕事もあるのだ。**無学な侍は奴隷だぞ。**奴隷のままで満足なのか？」。それからは、友は何も言わなかった。

　22歳になるまでに、藤樹の祖父母と父が亡くなった。そして近江に母を残すのみとなった。彼は学識と清廉な人柄でますます有名になったので、やがて豊かな報酬と名誉を与えられるのは間違いなかった。しかし、とにかく母のことだけを心配し、藩主のもとを去って母に仕える決心をした。彼は藩主にわびて、こう説明した。「殿は私のような家臣を何人でもお持ちになれますが、**私の老いた母には私以外に頼る者がいないのです**」。そして、自分の財産をすべて後に残し、母の家へと向かった。

all his free time reading. During those days, however, when the samurai's chief business was to fight, young Toju had to study secretly, only at night. But his secret was discovered. One day, one of his friends called him "Confucius," making fun of his nightly studies. "You idiot!" replied young Toju. "Don't insult Confucius by calling me by that saint's name. It makes me sad that you make fun of my love of knowledge. Poor fellow! The samurai's profession is not war alone, but the arts of peace as well. **An uneducated samurai is a slave**. Are you satisfied with being a slave?" The friend was silent from then on.

By the time he was twenty-two, Toju's grand-parents and father had passed away. He had only his mother left at Omi. As he grew more famous for his wisdom and purity of character, awards and honors were surely waiting for him. But he was only concerned for his mother, and he decided to leave his lord to serve his mother. He apologized to his lord and explained, "My lord can get any number of servants like me, but **my old mother has no one to depend upon except myself**." Then he made his way to his mother's home, leaving behind all his

母のそばに落ち着くと、藤樹は質素な生計を立てはじめた。持っていた金で酒を買い、村で売り歩いた。さらに、刀──「侍の魂」──も売ってしまい、銀十枚を手に入れた。これを村人たちにわずかな利息で貸し付けた。つつましい暮らしの小家族を支えるには、これで十分だった。藤樹はこのような卑しい仕事をしていても、恥ずかしいとは思わなかった。母を笑顔にできることが、ただうれしかった。

　2年間、藤樹はこのように暮らしていた。彼の著作から推測すると、この2年が人生でもっとも幸福な時だったらしい。**彼の目には、まったく無欲な人間になることが、学者や思想家になることより偉大だったのだ**。しかし、世間は学者としての彼をも必要としていた。そしてついに説得されて、その知識を人々のために用いるようになったのである。

possessions.

Once by his mother's side, Toju set about making a modest living. He bought some saké with the money he had and sold it around the village. He also sold his sword—"the samurai's *soul*"—and got ten pieces of silver for it. This he lent to the villagers at a small interest. This was enough to supply the little family with a humble existence. Toju did not feel shame in these low tasks. He was simply happy to be able to make his mother smile.

For two years he lived like this. From what we gather from his writings, these were some of the happiest years of his life. **Being a perfectly selfless man was grander in his eyes than being a scholar and philosopher.** But the world needed him as a scholar as well, and he was finally convinced to give his knowledge to the public.

第3節

近江の聖人

藤樹書院
藤樹の自宅で開かれた私塾。藤樹の死後は彼をまつる祠堂となった。

　28歳のとき、藤樹は村に学校を開いた。彼の家が寄宿舎であり、教室でもあった。その頃は、科学も数学も教えなかった。科目は、中国の古典、歴史、詩、そして書道だけである。学校経営による利益も、ささやかなものだった。**教職とは、富と名声を求める者たちからは軽蔑される仕事なのである。**

　この国の小さな村で、藤樹は静かに平和に暮らした。彼は名声を何よりも嫌った。**彼にとっては、自分の心が王国であり、他には何もいらなかったのである。**だが村の問題にはよく関わり、たとえば、村人が役人に訴えられると助けてやったりした。また農民や労働者に「人の道」を教えた。そして、**これらのささやかで親切な行為を、名声や評価を求めずに行なった。**「君子は日々、自分にやってくる小善を進んで行う」と彼は書いている。「もし大善に出会えばこれも行なうが、名声のために大善を求めない。大善は名声を生

III.
The Saint of Omi

When he was twenty-eight years old, he opened a school in his village. His house served as a dormitory and a lecture hall. Back then, no science or mathematics was taught. The Chinese classics, history, poetry, and handwriting were the only topics. The profits of running of school were modest too. **Teaching is a job despised by men who want fame and fortune**.

In that humble part of the country, Toju's life was quiet and peaceful. He hated fame more than anything. **To him, his mind was his kingdom**, and he needed nothing else. But he was very involved in village affairs, helping a villager, for example, when he was being tried at court. He taught the farmers and laborers the "ways of man." **He did these little acts of kindness without looking for fame or recognition.** "The *kunshi* gladly does the small deeds that come to him every day," he wrote. "He also does great deeds if they come his way, but

むが、小善は徳を生む。世は名声と威信を好むので、大善を求める。しかし、大善が名声や威信のためだけに行なわれるなら、その大善は小善になる」

　彼の教えには独特な点が1つあった。**知的な成績よりも、徳や性質を重視したのである。**真の学者についての彼の考えを以下にあげよう。

　「『学者』というのは、学問ではなく、徳を持つ者の名である。文学は学問であり、その才能のある者はたやすく文学者になれる。しかし、徳がなければ学者ではない。文学を知っている凡人である。**無学でも徳のある者は凡人ではない。文学を知らない学者である**」

　何年もの間、教師は村外の誰にも知られることなく、静かで質素な生活を送っていた。だが運命は藤樹を見出し、世に広く知らしめたのである。それはこのようにして起こった。

　岡山出身のある若者が、偉大な先生を求めて国じゅうを旅していた。近江を通りかかったとき、ある宿に泊まった。隣の部屋には2人の旅人がいた。1人の侍がもう1人に話しているのが、

he does not seek them out for fame's sake. Great deeds create fame, but small deeds make *virtue*. The world seeks great deeds, because it loves fame and prestige. However, if a great deed is only done for fame and prestige, the great deed becomes small."

One thing was peculiar in his teaching. **He prioritized virtue and character over intellectual achievement**. Here is his idea of a true scholar:

"'Scholar' is a name for virtue, not for arts. Literature is an art, and a man with a genius for it easily becomes a literary man. But he is not a scholar if he lacks virtue. He is an ordinary person who knows literature. **An illiterate man with virtue is not an ordinary person. He is a scholar without literature.**"

For years, the teacher led a quiet, simple life, unknown to anyone outside his village. But Fate discovered him and introduced him to the world. This is how it happened:

A young man from Okayama was traveling the country to find a great *sensei*. As he traveled through Omi, he stopped at a hotel for a night. In a room next to his were two travelers. The young

ふと若者の耳に入った。

「私は主君に命じられて江戸へ行ってきた」と彼は言った。「そして主君の数百両の金を運ぶよう任された。いつもは肌身離さず持っていたのだが、この村に着いた日は、その日に雇った馬の鞍に財布をくくりつけていた。宿に着くと、私は鞍にくくりつけた大金のことを忘れたまま、馬と別当（馬子）を帰してしまった。金を失くしたことに気づいたのは、しばらくしてからだ。私は打ちのめされた。別当の名前を知らなかったから、捜し出すこともできない。たとえできても、彼がすでに金を使ってしまっていたら、どうしたらいいのか？　忘れたことは弁解しようがない。だから、**面目を保つためにできる唯一のことは、主君にお詫びして死ぬことだった**。私は手紙を用意し、死ぬ覚悟をした。

すると夜中に、誰かが私の部屋の戸を叩いた。驚いたことに、それは雇った馬の別当だった。『お侍さま。この財布を鞍にお忘れでしたよ。家に着いてから見つけたので、お渡しするため引き返してきたのです』と彼は言った。私は飛び上がらんばかりに喜んだ！『おまえは命の恩人だ。どうかこの金の4分の1を受け取ってくれ』と私

別当（馬子）
馬の背に貨物や人を乗せて運ぶ輸送業。別当自身は徒歩。

man overheard one samurai telling the other a story.

"I went to the capital on an errand for my lord," he said, "and I was trusted to carry several hundred pieces of my lord's gold. I usually carried them close to my body, but on the day I reached this village, I tied the purse to the saddle of the horse that I had hired for the day. I reached my hotel, and forgetting the treasure on the saddle, I sent the horse away with its *betto*. I realized my loss several hours later. I was devastated. I didn't know the name of the *betto*, and I couldn't seek him out. Even if I could, what could I do if he had already spent the gold? There was no excuse for my forgetfulness, so the **only honorable thing I could do was to apologize to my lord and die**. I prepared letters, and I prepared for my death."

"At midnight, somebody knocked at my door. I was amazed to see it was the *betto* whose horse I had hired. 'Sir Samurai:' he said, 'You left this purse on the saddle. I found it after I reached my home, and I came back to give it to you.' I was overjoyed! 'I owe my life to you,' I told him. 'Please, take a fourth of this gold.' But the *betto* refused! 'You don't

は言った。ところが、別当は断ったのだ！『私は恩人などではありません。これは、もともとあなたの財布ですから』。それで私は15両を渡そうとし、それから5両、2両、最後には1両を渡そうとしたが、無駄だった。とうとう彼が言った。『私は貧乏なので、わらじを一足買ってください。この大切な用のために10マイル歩きましたから』。彼が背を向けて行こうしたとき、私は呼び止めて尋ねた。『どうか教えてくれないか。**どうしてそれほど無欲で、正直で、誠実でいられるのだ**。これほどの正直さは見たことがない』。すると、『私どもの小川村には、先生が住んでおられるのです』と貧しい男が答えた。『お名前は中江藤樹さまです。先生は、**人生の目的は自分ひとりの利益ではなく、誠実と正義だ**とおっしゃいます。村の者は先生の話を聞き、その教えに従って暮らしているのです』」

若者はその話を聞いていた。「これこそ、私が探し求めていた偉大な学者だ」と彼は言った。「その人のところへ行き、弟子にしてもらおう」

その若侍は藤樹の弟子になった。名前は熊沢蕃山といい、のちに強大な岡山藩の財政と行政を任されるようになった。そして自分の国に、後世まで残るような素晴らしい改革をたくさん採

owe me anything. The purse is yours.' I tried to give him fifteen pieces, then five pieces, two pieces, and finally one piece, without success. At last, he said, 'Because I am a poor man, please buy me a pair of straw sandals, as I walked 10 miles for this special purpose.' When he turned to go, I stopped him and asked, 'Please, tell me **what makes you so unselfish, honest, and true**. I've never seen such honesty.' 'In my village of Ogawa lives a teacher,' the poor man answered. 'His name is Nakae Toju. He says **personal gain is not the aim of life, but honesty and righteousness**. We villagers listen to him and live by his teachings.'"

The young man heard the story. "Here is the great scholar I seek," he said. "I will go to him and become his student."

The young samurai became Toju's *deshi*. His name was Kumazawa Banzan, the future financier and administrator of the powerful Okayama clan. He introduced many good and lasting reforms in

り入れたのである。

　藤樹の静かな生活についての話を終える前に、もう1つだけ触れておきたいことがある。西洋の読者諸君は、この教師と妻との関係について知りたいと思うだろう。藤樹は、厳格な一夫一婦主義者だった。30歳のときに結婚したが、妻となった女は美しくなかった。彼の母は再婚するよう勧めた——これは、当時そうした状況ではよくあることだった。だが、母の言うことはほとんどなんでも聞く藤樹が、これだけは断った。彼は言った。「たとえ母上のお言葉でも、天の法に反することは、お聞きするわけにはまいりません」。それで、妻は生涯彼とともに暮し、2人の子を産んだ。彼女は、「夫が誉れを受けられるよう、自分の誉れはすべて犠牲にする」典型的な日本の妻だった。**この心の美しさのゆえに、藤樹にとって理想的な女性となったのである。**

his land.

I have one more thing to mention before we close this part of his quiet life. Western readers would like to know the teacher's relation to his wife. Toju was a strict monogamist. He was married at thirty, but the woman he married was not pretty. His mother suggested remarriage—this was common under such circumstances. But Toju, who listened to almost everything his mother said, refused. He said, "Even a mother's word should not be respected if it goes against Heaven's laws." So his wife stayed with him all her life, gave birth to two children, and was one of those typical Japanese wives "who avoid all honors so that their husbands may be honored." **It was this spiritual beauty of hers that made her his ideal woman**.

第4節

内面の人

物質的に簡素な生活とは正反対に、藤樹の心や精神はとても豊かだった。彼にとって、心は自分が王として支配する王国だった。今日、彼の著作が10冊残っているので、その心の内を見ることができる。

これらの本を見ると、藤樹の知性の形成には2つの段階があったことがわかる。第1段階では、保守的な朱子学の影響を受けた。当時、彼を含めすべての男子が、朱子学の教えのもとに育てられたのだ。朱子学では、**常に自らを探求することが重視された**。第2段階は、進歩的な中国人、王陽明による影響である。**陽明は孔子の教えを進歩的に解釈し、それに基づいて教えをまとめあげた**。実際的な藤樹はこれを見て、自分なりの陽明主義をいくつか書いている。

朱子学
中国、南宋の朱子によって集大成された儒教の新しい思想体系。

王陽明
1472-1529、中国みん時代の儒学者、思想家。朱子学を批判的に発展させた陽明学を起こした。

「進み続けよ、道が暗くても。
　　　仕事がすむ前に空が明るくなるだろう」
　（暗くともただ一向にすすみ行け心の月ははれ

IV.
The Inward Man

Toju's simple material life was the opposite of his mental and spiritual riches. For him, his mind was a kingdom over which he ruled as a king. Today, we have ten volumes of his writings, which reveal his soul to us.

These books show us that his intellectual career had two phases. The first was influenced by the conservative Chu philosophy. He and all men of his time were brought up under these teachings, which **emphasized constant examination of one's self**. The second phase was influenced by the progressive Chinese, Wang Yang Ming. **Yang Ming interpreted the teachings of Confucius in a progressive way and built upon it.** Toju, a practical man, saw this and wrote some of his own Yang-Ming-isms:

"Keep pressing on, though your way is dark;
Skies may clear before your work is done."

やせんもし）

「心の糸を強く引き締めよ、
　　　長く苦しい行進に備えよ」
（志つよく引立むかふべし）

　藤樹の著作はまた、人の作った法律（法）と、永遠の真理（道）の違いを明らかにしている。彼はこう述べた。「**道と法は別のものである。法は、たとえその国の賢人が作ったとしても、時とともに変化する。しかし道は永遠に変わらない。**法はその時代の必要に合うように作られる。時と場所が変わり、世に押しつけられれば、たとえ賢人の法であっても道を損なう」

　とはいえ**藤樹にとって、謙譲ほど大切なものはなかった。**それは他のあらゆる徳を生じさせる徳だと、彼は信じていた。謙譲がなければ、何も持たないのと変わらない。「学者がまず自分を虚にして謙譲の徳を求めないならば、たとえ多くの教養と才能があっても、まだ卑しい者にすぎない」と彼は言った。

　この謙譲、つまり「虚」を達成するために、藤樹の用いた方法は単純だった。「**有徳であれ。日々、ただ善を行なえ。**1つの善を行なえば、1つ

"Tightly pull your heart's string,

   Prepare for a long, hard march."

Toju's writings also make clear distinctions between man-made Laws (法) and eternal Truths (道). He said, "The truth and the law are different things. **The law changes with time, even with wise men in their land. But the truth is eternal**. The law was made to meet the needs of the time. When time and place change, even wise men's laws harm *truth* if they are forced upon the world."

Despite this, **nothing was more important to Toju than humility**. He believed it was the virtue that gave rise to all other virtues. Without it, a man had nothing. "Unless the scholar first empties himself to seek the virtue of humility, he is still a lowly man, even with all his education and genius," he said.

To attain this humility, or "emptiness," Toju had a simple method. "**To be virtuous, simply do good day by day**. One good done, and one evil goes. **Do**

の悪が去る。**日ごと善を行なえば、日ごと悪は消え去る。**昼が長くなれば、夜が短くなるのと同じである。たゆまず善を行なえば、悪はすべて消え去るであろう」と彼は言った。

　このわかりやすい哲学により、藤樹は一生を通じて人生を楽しんだようである。彼が書いた次の和歌に注目してみよう。

　「少しも知らなかった、

　　　この苦しく悲しい人生を、

　　学問の助けによって、

　　　いつまでも平安に暮らせるとは」

（思いきやつらくうかりし世の中を学びて安く

　　楽しまんとは）

　残念なことに、藤樹は長寿に恵まれなかった。1648年の秋、40歳でこの世を去った。村じゅうの人々が彼の死を悼んだ。葬儀は国をあげて行われた。藤樹の家は今日まで残っており、墓を訪れると村人が案内してくれる。その人に、なぜ300年も前に生きていた人をそれほど敬うのか尋ねたら、彼はこう答えるだろう。

　「この村では、父は子に優しく、子は父に従順

good daily, and evil disappears daily. Just as the day grows long and the night grows short, if we persevere in good, all evil will disappear," he said.

With these simple philosophies, Toju seemed to have enjoyed his life thoroughly. Consider this poem he wrote:

"I knew little that this life,
　　　　With all its difficult sorrows,
　　Could by education's kind help,
　　　　Be spent in endless peace."

Sadly, Toju did not enjoy his life long. In the autumn of 1648, when he was forty years old, he passed away. The whole village mourned his death. His funeral was a national event. His house still stands to this day, and when you visit his grave, a villager will guide you. Ask him why such respect is paid to a man who lived three hundred years ago, and he will answer:

"Here in this village, the father is kind to the

で、兄弟は互いに親切です。家で怒声が聞かれることもなく、みんな平和に暮らしています。これはすべて、藤樹先生の教えのおかげなのです」

son, the son is loyal to the father, and brothers are kind to one another. In our homes no angry voices can be heard, and we are all peaceful. We owe all this to the teachings of Master Toju."

日蓮上人
仏僧

Chapter 5
SAINT NICHIREN
A Buddhist Priest

第1節

日本の仏教

　宗教は人間にとって主要な関心事である。**簡単に定義すると、宗教は人生に対するその人なりの解釈である。**そして、この悲しみの世に慰めをもたらすために、誰もがなんらかの解釈を必要としている。

　宗教はまた、死の問題——私たちすべてにやってくる、答えようのない問題——にも取り組む。死んでも死なないこと——これがすべてのキリスト教徒の望んでいることであり、日本人も同じである。**日本人にとって、死はとくに辛いものとされてきた。というのも、この美しい国から離れたくないからだ。**春を輝かせる桜、秋を彩る紅葉など、人生には楽しいことが多くある。だから、運命や義務によって最愛の母国から取り去られるとき、慰めとなる宗教が必要なのだ。

　日本人にはもともと独自の宗教があったが、これはおそらく古代に中央アジアからもたらされたものだろう。しかしやがて、インドからやってきたもっと複雑な宗教に取って代わられた。仏教で

神道
日本固有の民俗信仰。自然崇拝やあらゆる事物に霊魂が宿ると信じる観念（アミニズム）が特徴。

I.

Buddhism in Japan

Religion is humanity's main concern. **Defined simply, a religion is a person's own explanation of life**. And, everybody needs *some* explanation to provide some comfort in this world of sorrows.

Religion also addresses the question of death—that unanswerable question that comes to us all. *To not die by dying*—this is what all Christians hope for, and the Japanese too. **To the Japanese, death has been especially painful because we do not want to leave our beautiful land**. With the cherry blossoms brightening our spring, and the maples painting our autumn, life has often been pleasant. So, we need religion to comfort us when fate or duty takes us away from our beloved homeland.

The Japanese have their own religion, which was probably brought from Central Asia in ancient times. But this has been replaced by a much more complex religion that came from India: Buddhism.

ある。

欽明天皇
509–571、第29代天
皇。

仏教は欽明天皇の治世の13年目、西暦552年
頃に日本へ伝わった。その次の世紀に、天皇た
ちは積極的に民を仏教徒に変えた。学者が中国
へ送られ、玄奘のもとで学んだ。玄奘は、仏教を
学ぶためにインドまで旅をした有名な僧である。
奈良時代（708年〜769年）の天皇たちは、彼ら
の建てた偉大な寺が示すように、仏教の強力な
後ろ盾となった。

玄奘三蔵
602–664、中国唐時
代の僧。法相宗の
開祖。

最澄
767–822、平安時代
の僧侶。天台宗の
開祖。

空海
774–835、平安時代
の僧侶。弘法大師
として知られる真
言宗開祖。

仏教8宗
三論、法相、華厳、
律、成実、倶舎、
天台、真言の8宗。

紀元788年、仏教学者の最澄が京都の近くに延
暦寺を建て、紀元816年に、空海が有名な東寺を
建てた。その頃から、**日本の仏教は国内にしっか
りと根付いた**のだった。9世紀の初めには、「仏教
8宗」が栄えていた。そして4世紀の間に「8宗」
は力と影響力を増した。当然、このために腐敗す
るところもあったが、12世紀の終わりまで改善
されることはなかった。

既存の宗派の虚飾や尊大さに嫌気がさし、
1200年、仏教の禅宗が中国から持ち込まれた。大
きな禅寺が京都、鎌倉、越前に建てられ、新しい
教えを広めた。上流の知識階級の人々はこの新

Buddhism was introduced into Japan in the thirteenth year of the reign of Kinmei, around the year 552 of the Christian era. In the next century, emperors actively converted their people to Buddhism. Scholars were sent to China to study under Xuan Zhuang, the famous priest who traveled to India to study Buddhism. The emperors of the Nara dynasty (708–769) were all strong supporters of Buddhism, as their mighty temples show.

In 788 AD, the Buddhist scholar Saicho established Enryakuji near Kyoto, and in 816 AD, Kukai founded the famous Toji temple. Since that time, **Japanese Buddhism was rooted firmly in the land**. By the beginning of the ninth century, the "eight sects of Buddhism" were thriving. For four centuries, the "eight" grew in power and influence. This, of course, led to corruption in some quarters, yet there were no reforms until the end of the twelfth century.

Tired with the pomp and arrogance of the existing sects, the Zen school of Buddhism was introduced from China in 1200. Great temples were built in Kyoto, Kamakura, and Echizen to spread

しい教えを好んだが、庶民はそうではなかった。あまり教育を受けていない労働者階級の人々には、近づきやすい宗教が必要だった。そこで、源空（法然）と呼ばれる僧が、そういう宗教を庶民に与えた。浄土宗、つまり「極楽浄土」の教えを伝えたのである。

源空
1133–1212、平安末期の僧侶。比叡山で諸宗を学び、浄土宗を開いた。

浄土宗は、ただ仏の名を唱えるだけで、人は極楽浄土へ行けると教えた。やがて念仏宗、つまり、仏の名を念じる宗派と呼ばれるようになった。「南無阿弥陀仏」（我が身をあなたにゆだねます、ああ、阿弥陀仏よ）という詠唱が、鈴を振る音楽にあわせて唱えられ、ときには踊りを伴うこともあった。

範宴
1173–1263、鎌倉時代の僧侶。浄土真宗の開祖。

この分派が真宗で、範宴（親鸞）という僧によって始められた。この宗派の特徴のひとつは、僧から貞節の誓い（一生不犯）を取り除いたことであり、僧たちはふつうの生活の喜びを味わえるようになった。このように仏教がわかりやすくなったので、庶民階級にも取り入れられるようになり、真宗は他のどの宗派より大きく成長した。

12の宗派
1876年（明治9年）に黄檗宗が禅宗のひとつとして独立し、全13宗派となった。

このようにして、**13世紀は日本の仏教を形づくるうえで、最後にして最大の時期となったの**である。今日、日本には合わせて12の宗派があ

the new teaching. The upper and intellectual classes preferred this new faith, but the commoners did not. Without much education, the working classes needed a religion that they could access easily. A priest called Genku gave them such a faith with the introduction of the Jodo or "pureland" sect.

It taught that one could enter the Pure Land simply by calling upon the name of Buddha. It came to be called Nen-Butsu, or Call-on-Buddha sect. The chant "Nam-Amida-Butsu" (I commit myself to thee O thou Amitabha Buddha) was set to music on the hand-bell and sometimes combined with dance.

A branch of this was the Shin sect, started by a priest named Han'en. One feature of this sect was to remove vows of chastity from priests, leaving them free to participate in the common joys of life. In this way, Buddhism was simplified and adopted by the common classes, and this sect grew larger than all other sects.

So, **the thirteenth century became the last and greatest era to shape Japanese Buddhism**. Today, we have a total of twelve sects. Now, in this age of

る。科学の時代である今だからこそ、精神的な英雄に思いを馳せることで、私たちも信仰と自己犠牲を思い出せるかもしれない。

science, it may help us to recall a spiritual hero to remind us of faith and self-sacrifice.

第2節

生誕と出家

日蓮
1222-1282、鎌倉時代、安房の国（現在の千葉県）の僧侶。日蓮宗（法華宗）の開祖。

貞応1年（1222年）の春、安房の国にある小湊村の漁師の家に、1人の子どもが生まれた。少年は善日麿（よい太陽の子）と名付けられた。生まれた日に起きたという奇跡の物語がたくさんあるが、華々しくするための作り話だろう。しかし、生まれた日については話しておく価値がある。というのも、この若き僧は、生まれた日が自分の宗教的運命を表していると考えたからだ。その年は、**仏陀が涅槃に入った（入滅した）年の2171年後**だった。これは、光が東方に現れて暗闇を照らすと、仏陀が予言した年である。日付は旧暦の2月16日で、**仏陀が涅槃に入った15日の次の日**だった。このつながりが、我らが英雄にとってひじょうに重要だったのだ。

涅槃
仏教の最終目的である悟りの境地。また、釈迦の死を表す。

12歳のとき、両親は彼を僧にしようと決心した。そして近くの清澄寺へ連れていき、学識と徳の高さで有名な住職、道善のもとで学ばせた。師

道善
?-1276、清澄寺の住職、日蓮の師。

II.
Birth and Priesthood

On a spring day of the 1st year of Joo (1222), a child was born to a fisher's family in the village of Kominato in the province of Awa. The boy was named Zen-Nichi-Maro (Good-Sun-Boy). There are many stories of miracles that occurred at his birth, which we believe are colorful myths. But the date of his birth is worth mentioning, because the young monk considered it a sign of his religious destiny. The year was **the 2,171st after Buddha's entrance into Nirvana**. This was the year that the Buddha prophesied a light to appear to the *east of him* to shine through the darkness. The day was the 16th of the second month of the lunar calendar, **a day after the Buddha entered Nirvana, which was on the 15th**. These connections were very important to our hero.

When he was twelve years old, his parents decided he would be a priest. They took him to nearby Kiyosumi temple to study under the abbot

である住職は、この少年にとても感心した。4年間の修行を終えると、若者は16歳で得度して僧となった。蓮長という名を与えられ、住職は彼を自分の後継者に指名しようと考えはじめていた。だがその頃、若者は**心の内に葛藤を抱えて苦しんでおり**、そのために家を出ることになるのである。

Dozen, who had a reputation for his learning and virtue. The teacher was impressed with the boy. When the youth passed his four-year novitiate, he was consecrated as a priest at age sixteen. He was given the name of Rencho, and the abbot was beginning to consider nominating him as his possible successor. But, at this time, the youth **experienced inner struggles** that drove him away from home.

第3節

暗黒の内と外

　仏教を学んでいると、蓮長の心にいくつかの難しい問いが生じてきた。「なぜ仏教は今、これほど多くの宗派に分かれているのか？」と彼は問うた。「もともとは1人の人の教えから始まったのだ。**なぜ1つの宗派が、他のすべての宗派を悪く言うのだろう？　そして、どの宗派も自分の宗派が仏陀の本当の教えだと言うが、なぜそう言い切れるのか？**　これらの宗派のうちで、いったいどれが仏陀の道——私の従うべき道——なのだろう？」

　誰も、住職でさえも、彼の質問に答えられなかったので、彼は勉強と祈りに打ち込んだ。ある夕べ、涅槃経を読んでいると、次の1節が目を引いた。真理に頼み、人に頼るな（依法不依人）。この意味は、人の意見がどれほどもっともに聞こえても、それに頼るな、ということである。**すべての問題は、仏陀の経典によって解決されるべきである**。この言葉が、彼の悩める心を静めた。

III.

In and Out of Darkness

As Rencho studied Buddhism, several troubling questions arose in his mind. "Why is Buddhism now divided into so many sects?" he asked. "Its origin was in the teaching of one man. **Why does one sect speak badly of all others, and how can each insist that it follows Buddha's true teaching?** Which among these sects is Buddha's way—the way I should follow?"

Nobody, not even the abbot, could answer his question, so he turned to study and prayer. One evening, as he read the Nirvana Sutra, the following passage caught his attention: 依法不依人. *Trust in the Word and not in man.* This meant he was not to trust in human opinions, however reasonable they may sound. **All questions should be decided by the Buddha's sutras.** These words calmed his troubled mind.

しかし、仏教の経典はキリスト教の聖書のように単純ではない。聖書は1つしかないが、日本の仏教には十数冊の経典があり、教えが矛盾していることもよくある。若き僧は、複数の経典から「本当の教え」を選ばなければならなかった。

蓮長はこれを、大乗仏教、小乗仏教両方のすべての偉大な経典を、年代順に追っていくことで成し遂げた。この順番によれば、**妙法蓮華経**（または**法華経**）が、仏陀の人生における最後の8年間の教えを記していた。蓮長の下した結論は、**その最後の経典に、仏陀の全人生の教えの真髄が含まれている**、というものだった。この瞬間から、若き僧は妙法蓮華経を仏教信仰の規範としたのである。彼はうれし涙を流して泣いた。もう僧侶たちの言葉など聞かず、「仏陀自身の金言」に従おうと決心したのだ。そして20歳で住職に別れを告げ、真理を求めて当時の首都、鎌倉へ向かった。

しかし、蓮長は鎌倉で異様なものを目にした。美しい寺院がたくさんあるにもかかわらず、**町には偽りの教えと不正な行いがはびこっていた**のだ。禅宗が上流階級を、浄土宗が下層階級を導

大乗仏教
仏教を二分する一派。自分が悟りをひらくためだけでなく、すべての生き物を救おうという教え。

小乗仏教
従来の伝統仏教。自己の悟りの追求のみに偏重するという批判的な名称で、上座仏教ともいう。

教典の年代
華厳経、阿含経、方等経、般若経、妙法蓮華経の順番。

But Buddhist scripture is not so simple as the Christian. While there is only one Bible, the Japanese had dozens of sutras, often teaching contradictory things. The young monk had to select the "true teachings" from multiple volumes.

Rencho accomplished this by following the chronological order of all the great sutras in both Mahayana and Hinayana. According to this order, the **Sadharma-Pundarika Sutra (Myo-Ho-Renge or Hokke Kyo**) recorded the teachings of the last eight years of Buddha's life. Rencho's conclusion was that **the last sutra contained the essence of the teaching of Buddha's *whole* life**. From this moment on, the young monk held the Saddharma-Pundarika Sutra as the standard of the Buddhist faith. He cried tears of joy as he decided that he would not follow the words of priests, but only "the golden words of the Buddha himself." He was twenty years old when he said farewell to his abbot and went to Kamakura, the capital, to seek the truth.

However, in Kamakura he saw strange things. Despite all its beautiful temples, **the city was filled with false teachings and practices**. The Zen sect led the high classes, the Jodo sect led the low classes,

いており、仏陀の教えはどこにもなかった。僧たちの教えによれば、救いは阿弥陀仏の名前を繰り返し唱えることによって見出されるのであり、善行や修行によるのではないという。だから**人々は、南無阿弥陀仏と唱えながら、思うままに罪を犯していた。**

鎌倉で5年間すごした後、人々には新しい光の時代が必要だと、彼は確信した。「仏陀の予言した、地に信仰を取り戻す光とは、私のことだろうか?」。この思いを胸に、蓮長は鎌倉を去り、さらなる知識を得ようと叡山へ出発した。

比叡山延暦寺
滋賀県大津市に位置する、天台宗総本山。

過去千年にわたって、**叡山は日本の仏教学の中心となってきた。**ここで源空が学び、その弟子で、真宗の開祖である範宴が学んだ。そして今、我らが蓮長が、日本に真の仏教を広げようという野心に燃え、同じ山での悟りを求めて、400マイルの道のりを歩いてきたのである。

ここで古代の原典や注釈書に囲まれて、蓮長は仕事に取りかかった。彼の専門は妙法蓮華経だった。10年間、蓮長は叡山にとどまり、複雑な経典を研究した。そして今、**妙法蓮華経が他のどの経典よりも優れている**と確信したのである。

and Buddha's Buddhism could not be found anywhere. Holy men taught that salvation could be found by repeating the name of Amitabha, not by acts of virtue and discipline. Thus, **chanting Nam-Amida-Butsu, people were free to sin**.

After spending five years in Kamakura, he was convinced that the people needed a new era of light. "Am I the light that the Buddha prophesied to bring Faith back to the land?" With this thought, Rencho left Kamakura and set out for Eizan to gain further knowledge.

For the last thousand years, **Eizan has been the center of Buddhist learning in Japan**. It was here that Genku studied, and his student Han'en, the founder of the Shin sect. And now our Rencho, ambitious to spread genuine Buddhism in Japan, walked four hundred miles to seek enlightenment in the same mountain.

Here, surrounded by ancient texts and commentaries, Rencho set to work. His specialty was Saddharma-Pundarika Sutra. For ten years, Rencho stayed in Eizan, studying the sutra's complexities. He was now convinced that **the**

彼は京都でも研究を続け、奈良や高野山にも行った。あらゆる疑問が心から消え去ったとき、この経典のために自分の命を捧げようと、心の準備が整った。

そのとき、蓮長は32歳。友は1人もいなかったが、独立心にあふれ、意志は固かった。名声も、金も、有力な友もなく、目の前には困難な仕事が待っている。彼はたった1人で、あらゆる障害を乗り越え、当時影響力を持っていたすべての宗派に対立する見解によって、教えを広め始めた。彼の人生が興味深いのは、その教えのためではなく、**教えを守りとおした勇敢な方法**のためである。

Pundarika Sutra was superior to all the other Sutras. He continued his research in Kyoto, and also went to Nara and Koya. When every doubt was cleared from his mind, he was ready to lay down his life for the Sutra.

He was now thirty-two years old. He had no friends, yet he was independent and resolute. With no prestige, money, or powerful friends, he had a difficult task ahead of him. He began alone, against all odds, with a view that opposed all the influential sects of the day. His life is interesting not so much for his doctrines, as for **the brave way in which he upheld them**.

第4節

宣言

蓮長は教えを広めるのに、まず自分の村から始めた。質素な家に住み、名前を日蓮、つまり太陽の蓮、と改めた。建長5年（1253年）4月28日、日蓮は崖に登り、太平洋を見下ろして、祈りを唱えた。**他の祈りを沈黙させ、仏教の真髄を体現する祈り**だった。それは、南無妙法蓮華経、サンスクリット語で「ナマ・サッダルマ・プンダリーカヤ・スートラヤ」、その意味は「へりくだって白蓮の不思議な法の経典を信じます」である。

その日の午後、彼は初めて同胞たちに語りかけた。村人は、鎌倉や叡山や奈良で15年も学んできたこの僧に、すでに好奇心を抱いていた。そこで、老いも若きも、男も女も、こぞってやってきた。寺が人でいっぱいになると、日蓮は話しはじめた。まず、彼の経典、法華経の一部を読んだ。それからこう言った。

「私は何年もあらゆる経典を学び、さまざまな

蓮
仏教において、清浄さと智慧、慈悲を象徴する存在とされている。

IV.

Proclamation

To spread his knowledge, Rencho began at his own village. In his humble home, he changed his name to Nichiren, Sun-Lotus. On the 28th day of the fourth month of the fifth year of Kencho (1253), Nichiren climbed a cliff, looked down on the Pacific before him, and said a prayer. It was **a prayer to silence all others, to embody the essence of Buddhism**. It was *Nam-Myo-Ho-Renge-Kyo*, or, in Sanskrit, *Nama Saddharma-Pundarikaya Sutraya*, meaning "I humbly trust in the Sutra of the Mysterious Law of the White Lotus."

That afternoon, he spoke to his fellow men for the first time. Villagers were already curious about this monk who spent fifteen years studying in Kamakura, Eizan, and Nara. So they came, young and old, men and women. When the temple was filled, Nichiren began to speak. First, he read a part of *his* sutra, the Pundarika. Then he said:

"I spent years studying all the sutras, and I have

宗派が経典について述べたものをすべて読んだり聞いたりしてきました。経典のひとつに、こう書かれています。仏陀が涅槃に入った後の500年間は、多くの人が努力せずに成仏する。次の500年間は、深い瞑想によって涅槃に入り成仏する。それから経典を読む500年、さらに寺を建てる500年がやってくる。その後は、『真の法が隠される』500年で、人は成仏への道をすべて失う。私たちは今、この時代にいるのです。そして、仏陀による直接の教えからあまりに遠く離れて生きているので、**成仏する方法は1つしかありません**。その方法は、妙法蓮華経の5文字の中に含まれています……。浄土宗は地獄への道であり、禅宗は悪魔の教えです。真言宗は異端であり、律宗は国の敵です。**これは私自身の言葉ではありません。経典の中に見出したのです。**今は法華経を学ぶときであり、私はあなたたちを助けるために仏陀から送られた使者なのです」

　日蓮が話し終えると、聴衆は怒って大声をあげだした。彼は狂っていると言う者がおり、不敬の罪で厳しく罰するべきだと言う者もいた。集会に出ていた地主は、日蓮が寺を出るなり襲おうと企てた。しかし、日蓮の師である年老いた優

地主
東条景信のこと。阿波国（千葉県）で地頭を務めていた武将。念仏宗徒。

read and heard all that different sects have to say about them. In one of the sutras we are told that for 500 years after Buddha entered Nirvana, many will attain Buddhahood without any effort. For the next 500 years, they will enter Nirvana with deep contemplation. Then will come 500 years of sutra-reading, and another 500 years of temple-building. Then will be 500 years of 'the concealment of the pure law,' when all ways of enlightenment is lost to mankind. We are now in this era. And, living so far removed from the direct teaching of Buddha, **there is only one way to attain Buddhahood**. That way is contained in the five characters of *Myo-Ho-Renge-Kyo*…. The Jodo sect is a way to Hell, and Zen is the teaching of demons. The Shingon is heresy, and the Ritzu is an enemy of the land. **These are not my own words; I found them in the sutra.** Now is the time to study the Lotus Sutra, and I am the messenger sent by Buddha to help you."

When he finished, the audience cried out in anger. Some said he was insane, while others said his blasphemy should be punished severely. A land-owner who attended the meeting planned to attack Nichiren as soon as he left the temple.

しい住職が、2人の弟子に命じて、日蓮を無事に
その地から逃がしてやった。

But Nichiren's kind old abbot ordered two of his disciples to take Nichiren safely out of the district.

ひとり世に抗して

故郷で拒絶された日蓮は、「真理を広げるのに最適の場所」である首都の鎌倉へ向かった。そこで、わらで作った小さな小屋（草庵）に、法華経とともに住んだ。偉大な日蓮宗は、この草庵で始まったのである。身延寺、池上寺、そして国じゅうにある5千以上の寺もすべて、始まりはこの草庵と、この1人の男にあった。**偉大な仕事というのは、常にこうして生まれるものである。1つの不屈の魂があり、それに反抗する世間があるのだ。**

1年の間、彼は再び沈黙し、研究と瞑想にふけっていた。やがて、日昭という名の初めての弟子を得た。日昭は、はるばる叡山からやってきたのである。日蓮はひじょうに喜んだ。というのも、これで今や、人々の前に姿を現して命を捨てても、自分の教えがこの国から失われる心配がないからだ。そこで、1254年の春、**それまで日本では見られなかったものを始めた。辻説法である。**

人々に怒鳴られたり、からかわれたりしなが

日昭
1236-1323、鎌倉時代の僧侶。天台宗から改宗し、日蓮に師事した。

V.
Alone Against the World

Rejected at home, Nichiren went to Kamakura, the capital, "the best place for spreading the truth." There, he lived in a little straw hut with his Pundarika Sutra. The great Nichiren sect began in this hut. The temples at Minobu, Ikegami, and more than five thousand temples in the land all had their beginning in this hut and this one man. **This is how great works are always born: one unbreakable soul, and the world against him**.

For a year he was silent again, lost in study and thought. He got his first disciple, named Nissho, who came all the way from Eizan. Nichiren was glad, because he could now appear before the public and lay down his life without the fear of his doctrines being lost to his country. So, in the spring of 1254, **he began something Japan had never seen before: *street preaching***.

While the public yelled and jeered at him,

ら、日蓮は初めの宣言を繰り返した。不作法だと
非難する者がいると、戦時に全力を尽くすのは人
として正しいことだと答えた。天皇の宗教を悪
く言うべきではないと諭されると、「僧は仏陀の
使者だから、その仕事に恐れの入る余地はない」
と返した。また、他の宗派がすべて悪いはずは
ないと言われると、彼の簡潔な説明は、「足場は、
寺が出来上がるまで使われるだけだ」というもの
だった。6年間、雨の日も風の日もこのように説
教していると、**とうとう賛同する者が現れるよ**
うになった。彼の弟子のなかには、地位の高い者
——将軍家の者もいた。まもなく、彼が町じゅう
を改宗させるのではないかという恐れが生じた。

寺の住職たちは、日蓮の説法をやめさせよう
と画策したが、彼のことを見くびっていたよう
だ。日蓮は、最近この国で起きている多くの問題
を利用して、彼の最高の名著だとされている『立
正安国論』、つまり「民に平和をもたらす論」を
書いた。そのなかで、国が苦しむあらゆる災難を
列挙し、その**原因は偽りの教えにあると追及し**
た。その解決法は、国が最高の経典である法華経
を受け入れることである。もし受け入れなけれ
ば、内戦がおこり、外国の侵略を受けるだろうと

立正安国論
日蓮の代表的著
作のひとつ。1260
年、幕府で権力を
握る北条時頼へ上
呈された。

Nichiren repeated his first proclamation. When somebody accused him of indecency, he answered that it *was* decent for a man to do his utmost in a time of war. When he was told that he should not to speak badly of the emperor's religion, he replied, "The priest is Buddha's messenger, and fear has no place in his job." When somebody said that the other sects could not all be wrong, his simple explanation was that "the scaffold is only used until the temple is done." For six years he preached like this, in all weather, until **he began to gain a following**. Among his students were men of high rank—some in the Shogun's household. Soon, there was fear that he would convert the whole city.

Abbots planned ways to suppress Nichiren, but they underestimated him. Taking advantage of the land's many recent problems, he wrote what is considered his most remarkable work, *Rissho-Ankoku-Ron: A Treatise on Securing Peace for the People*. In it he listed all the ways the land was suffering and **traced their cause to false teachings**. The cure, he wrote, was the nation's acceptance of the highest sutra, the Pundarika. If not, he warned, the country would fall to civil wars and foreign

警告した。

　そのような言葉が語られたのは初めてだった。それは、**彼の宗派が倒れるか、もしくは他のすべての宗派が倒れるかという宣戦布告**だったのである。

invasion.

Such words had never been spoken before. It was **a declaration of war that could only lead to the fall of his sect, or the fall of all others.**

第6節

剣難、流刑、そして最後の日々

　　本を出してからの15年間、日蓮の生活は、**権力者たちとの絶えざる戦い**の日々だった。まずは伊豆へ3年間流された。すると彼は、そこの人々を改宗させた。鎌倉へ戻るとすぐ、危険も顧みず、再び説法を始めた。

　　ある夕べ、数人の弟子と旅をしていると、一群の武装した男たちに襲われた。その頭は、最初の宣言の後に日蓮を襲おうと企んだ例の地主だった。日蓮の弟子の3人が、師を守ろうとして殺された。こうして、法華経による日本での最初の殉教者が出たのである。日蓮は額に傷を負いながらも、かろうじて助かった。その傷は信仰のしるしとなった。

　　しかし、本当の危機は1271年の秋にやってきた。死罪を言い渡されたのである。それまで彼の命が奪われなかったのは、僧を死罪にすることが違法だったからである。だが国の支配者であ

VI.
Sword, Exile, and His Last Days

For fifteen years following the publication of his treatise, Nichiren's life was **a constant battle with the authorities**. He was first exiled to Izu for three years, where he converted the people there. As soon as he returned to Kamakura, he went back to his preaching, regardless of its danger.

One evening, when traveling with several of his disciples, he was attacked by a group of armed men. The leader of the group was the same landowner who had planned to attack Nichiren after his first proclamation. Three of Nichiren's disciples were killed in their effort to save their master. Thus the sutra had its first martyrs in Japan. Nichiren escaped with a wound on his forehead. It became a mark of his faith.

But the real crisis came in the autumn of 1271, when he was sentenced to death. So far, his life had been spared because it was illegal to execute a priest. However, Hojo, the ruler of the land,

北条時宗
12551–1284、鎌倉幕府第8代執権。彼の執事である平頼綱により日蓮は捕らえられた。

る北条氏は、日蓮の場合は特別だと決断した。

　その後に起こった事件は、日本の宗教の歴史において重要なものである。ただし事件に付随する奇跡のいくつかは、おそらく事実ではないだろう。伝えられた話によれば、死刑執行人が剣を振りかざすと、日蓮が経典の念仏を繰り返し唱えた。すると突然、天から一陣の風が吹き、剣は3つに砕け、剣士の手がしびれた。ちょうどそのとき使者が到着し、釈放の命令が鎌倉から届いたのだという。日蓮は救われたのである。

　日蓮は死罪のかわりに、再び流刑となった。日本海の孤島、佐渡へ送られた。そして流刑が終わるまでに、**佐渡の島民をすべて改宗させた**。このころには権力者たちも、日蓮の勇気と忍耐力に恐れと敬意を覚えるようになっていた。そして蒙古襲来——日蓮が外国による侵略として予言したもの——の脅威もあって、1274年、彼は鎌倉へ戻ることが許された。その後まもなく、**教えを国じゅうに自由に広めてもよいとの許可を与えられた**。日蓮はついに勝利したのである。

文永の役
1274年、モンゴル帝国（元）軍による日本侵攻。蒙古襲来。

　そのときには、この人も52歳になっていた。若い僧たちが熱心に教えを広めているので、日

decided Nichiren was a special case.

The event that followed is significant in the religious history of Japan, although some of the miracles attached to the event are probably not true. According to the story, when the executioner lifted his sword, Nichiren repeated sacred words from his Sutra. A sudden gust of wind came from heaven, the sword was broken into three pieces, and the swordsman's hand was paralyzed. Just then a messenger arrived, bringing an order of release from Kamakura. Nichiren was saved.

Nichiren was again exiled instead of being put to death. He was taken to Sado, a lonely island in the Japan Sea. By the end of his exile, **he had converted everyone on Sado**. By now, the authorities both feared and admired Nichiren's courage and perseverance. And, with the threat of a Mongol attack—which Nichiren had predicted in his prophecy of a foreign invasion—he was allowed to return to Kamakura in 1274. Soon after, **he received permission to freely spread his teachings across the land**. He had won at last.

The man was now fifty-two years old. With younger monks working to spread the word,

蓮は身延山に隠居し、弟子の教育と静かな瞑想のうちに最後の日々を送った。1281年に大きな蒙古襲来があり、自分の予言が当たるのを目にすることができた。もちろん、そのおかげで彼の名声はさらに上がった。翌年、弟子に招かれて池上へ行き、そこで世を去った。1282年10月11日のことである。

死の床でのある光景について話しておこう。最期を迎えた日蓮を慰めようと、人々が仏像を持っていったが、彼は手を振ってそれをどけさせた。そこで、妙法蓮華経の名が壮麗な漢字で書かれた掛物を目の前で広げた。すると日蓮は、掛物のほうにゆっくりと体を向け、手を伸ばしながら最期の息を引き取った。

弘安の役
1281年、二度目の蒙古襲来。どちらも暴風雨による戦艦の沈没に助けられ、撃退させた。

Nichiren retired to Mt. Minobu and spent his last days teaching and quietly contemplating. He lived to see his prophecy fulfilled in the great Mongol invasion of 1281, which of course increased his fame. The following year, he went to Ikegami as a guest of one of his disciples, and died there on the 11th day of the 10th month, 1282.

I will mention one scene from his death bed. They brought him an image of Buddha to comfort him in his last hours, but he waved it away. Then they unrolled before him a *kakemono* with the name of Saddharma-Pundarika Sutra written in magnificent Chinese characters. Toward this he slowly turned his body, and reaching his hands to it, he breathed his last.

人物評

　日蓮は、このエッセイ集の中でも、とりわけ謎めいた人物である。彼に敵対する人は、日蓮は不敬者で偽善者だと言う。彼は**仏教の悪いところをすべて身代わりとして負っている**のだ。キリスト教が日本にやってきたときも、やはり一緒になって彼を侮辱した。

　しかし、私は日蓮の人格を信じている。その教えは粗野だと批評できるし、もちろん語調も狂人のようである。彼は偏った人物で、一方向に突き進みすぎた。だが彼の魂はどこまでも誠実だった。もっとも正直な男で、もっとも勇敢な日本人だった。

　日蓮の勇気は、自分が法華経の使者だと信じていたことにある。「私は無価値な一介の僧侶にすぎません」と言ったことがある。「だが法華経に仕える者として、仏陀から遣わされた特使なのです」。彼にとって自分の命は重要ではなかった。ただ、**祖国が仏陀の教えを堕落させたので、国のために悲しんでいた。**もし彼が狂っていた

VII.
His Character

Nichiren is the most enigmatic character in this collection of essays. His enemies say he was a blasphemer and a hypocrite. He is **the scapegoat of all that is bad in Buddhism**. When Christianity made its appearance in Japan, it also participated in insulting him.

But I believe in this man. We can critique his doctrines as inelegant, and of course his tone was that of a mad man. He was an unbalanced character, pointed too much in one direction. But his soul was sincere to its core. He was the most honest of men, the bravest of Japanese.

Nichiren's courage was based on his belief that he was a messenger of the Pundarika Sutra. "I am a worthless, ordinary priest," he once said, "but as a servant of the Pundarika Sutra, I am Buddha's special messenger." His own life was not important to him, but **he grieved for his nation as it corrupted Buddha's teachings**. If he was demented, his

なら、その狂気は気高いものである。

　日蓮の私生活はとても質素だった。最初に鎌倉で草庵を建てた30年後、身延でもやはり同じような建物に住んでいた。また、彼が「仏陀の敵」と呼んだ相手には手厳しかったが、貧しく苦しんでいる者には穏やかで優しかった。弟子に宛てた手紙は、思いやりに満ちた言葉で書かれている。弟子たちが彼のことを心から慕ったのも不思議ではない。

　日本人の中で、日蓮ほど独立心にあふれた人物は他に思いつかない。その独立心と独創性によって、彼は仏教を日本の宗教とした。他の宗派がすべて、ヒンドゥーや中国や韓国の精神から始まったのに対し、**日蓮の宗派だけが純粋に日本的なものである**。彼は、受け身になりがちな日本人のなかで傑出していた。自分の意志を持っていたので、扱いにくい男ではあった。しかし、国の支柱となる人物はそういうものだ。日蓮は、その闘争心にもかかわらず、私たちが理想とする宗教者なのである。

しごう
諡号
日蓮の死後、1358年に「日蓮大菩薩」、1922年に「立証大師」の諡号が送られた。

dementia was a noble kind.

Nichiren's private life was very simple. Thirty years after he built his first straw hut in Kamakura, he was still living in a similar structure in Minobu. And although he was intolerant to what he called "Buddha's enemies," he was mild and kind to the poor and needy. His letters to his disciples are written in the softest of tones. No wonder they thought so much of him.

I cannot think of a more independent man than Nichiren among my countrymen. By his independence and originality he made Buddhism a Japanese religion. **Only his sect is purely Japanese**, while all others began in Hindu, Chinese, or Korean minds. He stood out among passive Japanese. He was a difficult man because he had a will of his own. But such is the nation's backbone. Nichiren, despite his fighter's spirit, is our ideal religious man.

[対訳ニッポン双書]

代表的日本人
Representative Men of Japan

2015年9月5日　第1刷発行

著　　者　内村　鑑三
英文リライト　ニーナ・ウェグナー
翻　　訳　牛原　眞弓

発 行 者　浦　　晋亮
発 行 所　IBCパブリッシング株式会社
　　　　　〒162-0804 東京都新宿区中里町29番3号 菱秀神楽坂ビル9F
　　　　　Tel. 03-3513-4511 Fax. 03-3513-4512
　　　　　www.ibcpub.co.jp

印 刷 所　株式会社シナノパブリッシングプレス

© IBC パブリッシング 2016
Printed in Japan

ISBN978-4-7946-0399-9